The Cards I was Dealt that Transformed my Life

Tracey Walker

 A catalogue record for this book is available from the National Library of Australia

Cover by Miriam Rudolph
Internal layout by Publishious

Disclaimer
Any opinions expressed in this work are exclusively those of the author and are not necessarily the views held or endorsed by others quoted throughout. All of the information, exercises and concepts contained within the publication are intended for general information only. The author does not take any responsibility for any choices that any individual or organization may make in relation to this information in the business, personal, financial, familial or other areas of life based on the choice to use this information. If any individual or organization does wish to implement the ideas discussed herein, it is recommended they obtain their own independent advice specific to their circumstances.

This book is available in print and eBook formats

Print: ISBN: 978-0-6456271-7-6

eBook: 978-0-6458010-1-9

DEDICATION

*To my son, Phillip, who challenged me to find
a solution, which ultimately led me on my own
journey of self-discovery to where I am today.
Thank you, Phillip.*

*To my challenges that uncovered my strengths.
These challenges have led me to living my passion and
fulfilling my dream of helping and supporting others to see
there is another way. I don't fight the difficulties today.*

*To the 12-Step Program for giving me a foundation to
work from and the steps I continue to take
to improve and evolve each day.*

*To all the positive people who supported me on the way.
I wish you all a prosperous and successful life.*

Thank you, all!

MY WHY

This book has been a dream of mine for a long time. It has now come to fruition.

The reason I wrote this book is twofold: it has helped me see how far I have come, and I wanted to share my story to help others.

As I wrote about the journey of my life's challenges I was in awe of how many things have happened to me and the lessons I learned on the way. I am not the same shy little girl I was back in the day. I have evolved into an inspiring and empowering woman who can stand up for herself. In everyday life, I come across people who want to control others. Now, I have a voice to speak up. I see so many people that are content to sit back and take it. I hope this book will help readers ask themselves their own questions about who they are and what they want for their life. Are there people in their life holding them back, putting a gag on them or undermining what they want to do?

I recall fighting back to try and be heard and that didn't work. That just made things worse.

There is a different way, and that is what I have figured out on my journey and why I want to share it with others.

I have faced many failures and roadblocks on the way. Yet, I persisted!

For me, failure is part of my journey. Failure is an opportunity to try doing things another way. I never gave up. I may have paused at times while another idea came to me, and that was okay.

What I have learned is that life is not about other people and what they do, it is about what I do.

That is the key to why I wrote this book.

My answers come from inside myself, not outside myself. Having a mentor who taught me the tools and techniques to work on me, and get to know me, has turned my life around. Trying to change others is not the answer.

If my book can help people to understand this concept, then it has done its job.

I love supporting people to see things through a different lens. In my earlier days, I only saw what my family, children, relationships and others did, hoping they would see what they were doing and change. I had it all wrong.

Everything I have done and become has come from within, not from outside of me.

My book tells my journey. I've reflected on lessons learned along the way to help the reader think about where they are at and what changes they may like to consider.

It is a stepping stone to something amazing if you desire to do the work.

People who choose to work with me are ready to do the work to reach their goals and fulfil their dreams.

I hope my readers are ready to take the next step towards their own success.

Let it begin with you!

MY STORY

I have had challenges throughout my life.

In my early days, I faced one struggle after another. I felt this was my life and I had to just deal with it. I convinced myself that others had it worse.

This was my thinking until I found a different approach. It transformed my life forever.

Altering my perception and how I viewed things sounds so simple. It wasn't. I had to completely change everything I knew about myself. One step at a time, I learned who I was as a person and what I wanted out of life, instead of what everyone else wanted me to be.

To truly transform my life, I knew I needed to take the steps that would get me to a place I had only dreamed of – knowing there was no guarantee it would all work out.

Family and friends worried I was caught up in some kind of cult because I was doing things that weren't 'the norm' and that made the people around me feel uncomfortable.

What I realised, however, is that *I* was comfortable doing things differently. It was everyone else that experienced the discomfort because they realised they couldn't push my buttons anymore.

I was taking back control of my life.

I finally felt I held the power and this encouraged me to continue exploring my new way of living. I began to like and respect myself. This was the 'new Tracey' and it was no longer important what others thought about me.

I had to believe it would all work out. Now, I know it was worth every step because it brought me to a life I love.

It's only the beginning – there is so much more for me to achieve and more success to be had in my lifetime.

At times, it was hard and scary. Doubts and fears would rise up and take me back to what I knew; to what was comfortable. I have walked that walk; I understand how hard it is for my clients to take that first step towards a new life.

My passion is to continue exploring what is possible.

I believe anything is possible.

And that belief stands true for all of us.

LIVING MY 'WHY'

I love what I do.

Using the same modalities that supported my healing from past imprints and limiting beliefs, I help my clients overcome their obstacles to success. Together we go deeper into clearing what holds my clients back, and they're amazed by what they learn about themselves. It is this learning that is so powerful. These are the tools I use in my everyday life.

Connecting with my smaller self has helped me to gain clarity on situations – imprints – that have an impact on my everyday life. Most people are unaware of these imprints or think they have dealt with their past or understand where emotions have come from. I personally know it's often not that simple, because every time I connect with my smaller self, using alternate modalities with a practitioner, the things that come to the surface for me blow my mind.

I love the journey I go on with my clients and passing on tools and strategies to my clients makes me feel alive. I love to hear my clients say, "Wow! Where did that come from?" The peace and freedom are powerful.

Everyone deserves a chance to go out into the world with confidence, to succeed and to achieve their dreams.

Everyone deserves to be empowered!

My personal journey has given me the skills to do what I believe I'm meant to be doing – helping people be the best they can be.

WHY THE BUTTERFLY?

The butterfly has a significant meaning in my business activities.

As I've learned a different way of thinking and doing, this is who I'm becoming – a butterfly; someone who went from something ordinary to something extraordinary. It all started with me taking that first step towards my fear, rather than away from it. Towards believing in something more for my life, even though I didn't know what 'more' looked like. I just trusted and believed it would all come together if I kept putting one foot in front of the other.

As I've evolved and crafted the person I want to be, I've slowly started to attract the people I want to become.

Spiritually, the butterfly symbolises spiritual rebirth, transformation, creativity, infinite potential, vibrant joy, change and an ability to experience the wonder of life.

This is my life. This is who I am. This is what I do.

TRACEY'S JOURNEY FROM ORDINARY TO EXTRAORDINARY

At what point does someone start to transform? What is their turning point; their stage of realisation? What is their catalyst for change?

Throughout my life I had many opportunities to go down a different path, but did I?

No.

I followed in my mother's footsteps – her exact footsteps. The generational cycle is not easy to break away from. It's comfortable. It's the only thing many people know. It was certainly the only way I knew how to live.

You cannot change something you're not aware of.

In the same way that gravity pulls you back to Earth, familiarity and fear of the unknown can pull you back to undesirable situations.

When I did reach the point where I started to think everything was wrong and that I should get out, I kept telling myself I couldn't do it on my own. It was so much easier to just fall into another relationship where someone would look after me and I didn't have to learn how to take care of myself.

Those thoughts are known as self-limiting beliefs. I'd carried them throughout my childhood and school years and, clearly, they were still impacting my choices as an adult. Except, at the time, it wasn't that clear.

I'd berate myself.

Why couldn't I move forward and create something different for my children? Would I be living the same life in fifty years?

My turning point was my children. There was the dull, but growing, thud of guilt that I was harming my children through my inaction, my fear of change.

The day my partner locked the door to our bedroom and beat me senseless was the day I finally realised. My children were out in the hallway, screaming. His mother looked at my bruises afterwards and simply said, "He's my son." Her face was slack. Passive. Unreadable. "I love him."

I didn't have anyone to help me.

Nobody.

I was on my own.

I had to help myself. I had to help my kids.

Things had to change. I had to make a start.

Joining a 12-step program for partners of alcoholics was a start.

Walking out on my second dysfunctional relationship was a huge step.

Returning to school to complete my education was another positive move.

Little by little, I began to break away. I began to change the inevitable. And I started to feel the generational mould crack and break away.

There were many times it would have been easy to give up. To stop and go back to what I knew. Sometimes I would fall back to what was comfortable, but I didn't stay there for long. I accepted that this was part of my growth and I knew I had to stay the course and see it through if I wanted something different.

Did I want something different?

Yes.

Did I want to be stuck on this merry-go-round for the rest of my life?

No. Not for me. Not for my children.

My children didn't need or deserve to live with what I had.

I persisted. I never gave up or gave in.

For my whole life, I had the power to change. It was a matter of changing my circumstances. It was not a case of changing my situation or the people around me. Those things contributed, but ultimately it was me.

Nobody else could change my life but me.

Now this is what I teach. This I what I help people do.

I don't want you to read my story and think, 'Poor Tracey.' I want you to read my story and have those 'aha' moments. I want you to make connections, however small.

Ultimately, I want you to realise that it is possible to change your life.

I had the power to change my course and so do you.

Inside this book is my life.

Inside this book are the cards I was dealt.

FOREWORD

The expression 'walk a mile in my shoes' echoes down the years and through the ages. It's an invitation to see things and events from someone else's point of view. Through the pages of this excellent book, you will walk more than just one mile in the shoes of another. In fact, you will cover many miles and have many experiences you may otherwise not wish to live through.

Tracey Walker was catapulted from an uncomplicated life as a young mother who never had to make any big decisions, into a situation where she had no choice but to grab hold of life with both hands and just do it. The lessons Tracey has learned along the way have made her the person she is today – respected and successful.

Adversity changes us. Whether the change is good or bad rests with us alone. Dealing with a string of tragedies, along with her childhood scars, forced Tracey to find an inner strength she never thought she had – a strength she now believes we all possess, if we know where to look.

As you walk alongside Tracey, you will recognise people you 'know' and you may also see yourself. You will come to realise a tragedy that 'only happens to someone else' could be just around the corner of your life's path.

Allow yourself to be drawn into Tracey's world and see how it's possible to take devastation and transform it into success. In doing so, realise that the life you are born into does not have to be the life you live – ordinary humans can become very special, successful and greatly respected people.

Read the book, enjoy the story. It will certainly make you think.

~ John Knox (Retired Brisbane Broadcaster) ~

CONTENTS

*Taking responsibility for your life and
choices is very empowering.*
~ Dr Wayne W Dyer ~

PROLOGUE

What a wild ride my life has been.

When I say 'wild', I don't necessarily mean it in the crazy and exciting sense but more in the sense it has been storm-like in its unpredictability. My life has not been smooth sailing. In fact, when I look back on everything I've been through, it is almost like watching a series of lives, loosely connected like slightly disjointed chapters in a novel.

Some people only deal with one major event in their lifetime.

Not me!

I've ricocheted from one event to another, with very little time in between to catch my breath and regroup.

It has been difficult. However, in writing this book, I can now see my life has been exactly what it was meant to be because it has brought me to this space. A space of exceptional awareness. I feel lucky to have had all these life experiences as they have given me the opportunity to be of service to others by virtue of having travelled the road my clients may be travelling. As my mentor Mary Morrissey stated:

No wind is favourable to the sailor who has no destination in mind.

Throughout my life, I never really had a destination in mind. I defaulted to what I knew – a roller-coaster ride of many ups and downs, but essentially travelling along a pre-determined path. It certainly hasn't been easy at times, but through the difficulty I have gained an empathy, compassion and insight other people may not have. I feel blessed to be able to connect with people who have been through similar circumstances.

Connections such as these are extremely powerful. They are my strength and I trust in the intuitive power that guides me to my higher self.

That higher self is with me every moment of every day, guiding me and giving me that nudge I need to continue climbing my Mt Everest of life.

Challenging times are when I know I grow the most. Growth is an awareness of 'me' and that is what my story is all about. Most people view the world from an outside-in perspective by looking at their circumstances and the situations happening to them.

I now live my life through me.

Change is going to come whether I like it or not. I can fight it or I can approach life straight on, rather than focusing on what is happening around and outside me. This is a powerful insight very few people understand.

I consider myself lucky because I didn't fear change, I embraced it.

Are you ready to take the path to self-discovery?

If so, jump in and join my journey. On the way, you will learn some lessons to help you take that quantum leap into the life you can have if you are open and willing to do things differently from how you have done them before.

Fear held me back for years. Don't let it be years for you. Change is possible – if you are ready and willing to take that first step without letting fear stand in your way.

Let it begin with you!

You are the most important person you will ever meet.

Get to know you.

It takes true strength of character to redefine
your limits by pushing past them.
~ Katherine Reutter ~

CHAPTER ONE
My Destiny-Changer

At the age of twenty-one, you think you are going to live a long and happy life. You dream of getting married, having children and living happily ever after. It's not always the case.

My husband and I were at a friend's housewarming party with our child. At one point, my husband started talking to one of the guests about motorbikes. My husband loved motorbikes and had his own. He'd asked the guy if he could go for a ride on his bike.

"You didn't get it up enough," the guy said when my husband got back. "Come for a ride with me."

"Sure. Let's do it," my husband said. They agreed to go out for a ride a bit later. I could see my husband was over the moon with excitement.

As the night went on, our two-year-old became tired so I took her to the bedroom to try and get her to sleep. I'd been sitting there for a while when my husband popped his head in to check if we were alright. "I'm heading off for that ride," he said.

It was the last time I saw him as I'd known him.

It was 27 July 1983 and everything I knew was about to come crashing down.

They must have been gone quite a while before the other guests started to become concerned. A few of them took off in their cars to have a look for them.

Then came the words no wife wants to hear: "There's been an accident."

I have no clear recollection of events from that point on. My mind was reeling with all these questions. Time had frozen and everything was running on autopilot. I don't recall getting to the hospital but someone must have taken me.

"My husband was brought in from a motorbike accident," I said.

Next thing I know, I'm looking at someone I didn't recognise. It was my husband but it wasn't the husband I knew. They'd cut off his clothes and shaved off his goatee and hair. Tubes protruded from his throat and nose. He was pale. There was blood. This wasn't my husband – it couldn't be.

"We're going to transfer him," someone said. A bigger hospital. More facilities. He'd be going by ambulance. With a police escort. They handed me a plastic bag. Inside, I saw his clothes – bloodied and cut.

This sort of thing happens to other people.

Words, images, sounds – everything was coming thick and fast. Too fast. My mind was whizzing like a computer, except nothing was computing and I didn't know what I was going to do.

Never for a minute did I think something like this was going to happen to me. Why would I? Yet, here it was, happening to me.

What was I going to do? I was turning twenty-one the following month. What a birthday present! I'd dropped out of school before I completed Year 9, so had no education to speak of – I'd failed myself. In hindsight, I realise I had choices but at the time I was following the only thing I knew – what I was born into – essentially, a violent, alcoholic environment with no encouragement to aspire to anything.

I had to step up.

As human beings, we have a natural instinct to survive and, suddenly, that instinct just kicked in. I knew that I would fight for his survival. I didn't want to be around anyone who had negative thoughts about my husband dying. It simply wasn't an option. Not on my watch. I was pregnant with our second child and had a two-year-old daughter – I was determined neither of them would grow up without a father. In a way, I was still a child myself and now I had to grow up very quickly.

I didn't know how I was going to do this but I couldn't accept any other outcome. My children needed a father and I needed a husband.

Sitting at the hospital, every day was long. They dragged on with nothing to do except watch for a sign; any small change to give me some hope. Who was this man I was visiting every day? He didn't look like the man I married, but all I knew was I had to fight for his survival. I wasn't ready to contemplate the alternative!

I soon realised my only real option was to go on the sole parent pension and for my husband to go on sickness benefits. Another thing I realised was that I didn't have a licence and was going to need one now. This meant overcoming my fear of failure and just doing the darn test. Fear had held me back from doing so much. It's strange how our thoughts automatically control our outcomes while we struggle with that internal dialogue.

The idea of being pulled over by the police without a licence terrified me. I had to step up. I had to face my fear of failure. I had to just do it.

I booked in.

The driving instructor had confidence in me. "You're an excellent driver," he said. "You'll pass with flying colours."

I did.

Over time, I got to know the nursing staff. They were like another family and were so supportive. New patients would come in and I'd hear their stories – football accidents, car accidents. It really was another world; while everyone else goes on with their lives, inside the hospital walls we were all waiting and hoping for a miracle. I truly felt for the parents of the children in the back of the ward. Many of the children had fallen off their bikes or a swing. I'd come in each day and discover they'd lost another child overnight. It was devastating. Nobody can know or understand the magnitude of the situation for so many families. The rest of the world does not hear or see anything. I was only one of so many families having to deal with their own devastation.

Families can be destroyed in an instant.

In that first twenty-four hours, my husband did stop breathing, but they brought him back. Seeing him on the ventilator and hearing that constant sound of him breathing – innnnnnn and outtttttttt, innnnnnnnn and outtttttttt – is something I'll always be able to hear. You can't forget it.

Our daughter didn't know what was going on. How can a two-year-old understand why her daddy had 'left'? Taking her to see him was so painful because he didn't look like her daddy. I would sit her on his bed and he'd moan and cry out. It was my husband, but he was trapped inside this unrecognisable body and screaming to be released.

Brain scans and tests showed there were spinal injuries and very little brain activity. This was no surprise – he'd landed on his head. He'd slid the entire length of a vacant block. I can't bear to imagine what must have been going through his head in that moment. We've all seen the movies where this sort of thing happens in slow motion. Still, despite these scans, I fought for the miracle that he would come through this and our life could go back to what it was before the accident. I fought to stay positive, even when others only saw the worst scenario.

Death!

It wasn't an option as far as I was concerned but it was still there, sitting in the back of my mind, that little voice saying it was a possibility.

The day came when they decided to take him off the ventilator to see if he could breathe on his own. "He'll either start breathing on his own or he'll pass away quietly," the doctor said.

Was I ready to face the world as a widow and single mother to two small children?

My answer was a resounding NO.

What if …? What would I do? How could I go forward and raise these children on my own? Why am I the one having to carry this load? Why am I the one having to pick up the pieces? How is this fair? How can I make all these decisions by myself? Why didn't I die? Why didn't we die together?

My mind was a mess of unanswered questions.

Death is easy. It's the people left behind that have it hard.

I held my breath as the doctors and nurses started the process of removing all the tubes from down his throat, except for the feeding tube in his nose. I waited for what seemed like hours. Everything was happening around me. Everyone was waiting for my husband's first breath.

Waiting and waiting.

Then it came! He took a breath.

Again, the realisation hit me hard. Here I was, pregnant and with a two-year-old; my husband was alive but in intensive care with brain and spinal injuries. Never had I been required to stand on my own two feet and make decisions that impacted anyone. It had always been easier to have someone else make those decisions while I tagged along. That had been my answer to everything – until now.

This was just the beginning of a new beginning. Another long journey.

Intensive care was no longer needed now that he was breathing on his own, so they moved him to a normal ward and started rehabilitation.

The next three months was like the movie *Groundhog Day* – the routine was the same every day. I'd drive to the hospital and sit with my husband, talking to him and massaging his hands and feet. Doctors and nurses buzzed around on their daily routines. They'd whisk my husband off for regular scans to see if anything had changed. Nothing ever did.

Friends and family found it hard because he wasn't the same person they remembered. He looked different. They couldn't communicate with him. Over time, fewer and fewer people came to visit. I understood why but it was still hard.

During rehabilitation sessions they would attach my husband to a tilt bed. He'd be strapped on and the bed would then be tilted to a vertical position – it was supposed to help extend his legs and arms to stop him curling up into a fetal position. "He'll work harder if you're there," the physiotherapist told me. "He'll know. It'll help."

I'm not in the medical profession, but I can't say I saw a lot of improvement over those three months. And honestly, I don't know where I found the strength to go back every day and watch this man deteriorate.

"He'd be better off dead," people – family – told me.

"He's going to die," I was told, again by family. "You need to prepare for that."

I suppose, looking back on my life, I've never been a person to give up. I may change tack and go in a different direction, but I've always believed there must be an answer for everything.

This was no different.

After a period, the doctors made the decision that he needed to be transferred to another hospital. I didn't really know why, but it was closer for me to travel so I was okay with that.

It wasn't quite what I expected.

The ward was full of people who had been in some type of accident – and they were all in a coma. I met parents who had been praying, wishing and hoping their child would one day wake up. They showed me photos from before the accidents – beautiful, vibrant people – and now they just lay in these beds doing very little. Some had been there for years.

"Your husband could live in this vegetative state well into his seventies" the doctor said.

It was like getting a punch in the guts. I was devasted. Up until the doctor said those words, I'd always believed my husband would come out of his coma. I believed that if I put all my love and care into this man and fought for his survival, he would come back to his family, back to his children.

I got in my car and drove to my sister's house. I have no idea how I got there and, to this day, I still don't know how I made it there without having an accident. My mind was reeling. This was not possible. I felt totally alone. Abandoned.

What now?

Every day became a seesaw of emotions – one moment I had hope, and the next I was waiting for the call to tell me he was gone.

Groundhog Day continued. I'd get up, settle our daughter with my mum and spend the day at the hospital. Then I'd come home, have dinner and answer messages from people wanting to know how my husband was doing.

What was I supposed to say to everyone when he was the same day in and day out?

If I told them the truth, would they stop asking? I didn't have any answers – not the ones they wanted to hear, anyway. All the pressure was on me.

What about the new baby? When I had the baby – what then? How could I raise a newborn and be at the hospital every day? What if this dragged on for years and years? I had an entire lifetime ahead of me, yet I didn't have a life. Nobody would want to take me on. I was on my own.

Was this my future?

Each day, my husband curled further up into a fetal position. What must it have been like for him, locked in his body and unable to do anything? I couldn't even imagine the fear he must have felt. Wanting to be a father and do what fathers do but unable to.

When the phone rang one morning, I knew it was bad news. I didn't want to come out of my room. I found every reason possible to stay right where I was. The inevitable had happened. What was I going to do now? What was I going to tell our daughter? "Daddy's gone to heaven." How can a two-year-old understand that concept? I didn't even understand it.

I was truly on my own, now. Nobody to discuss options with. Nobody to blame. If I stuffed things up, it was all on me.

How many people have to organise a funeral at the age of twenty-one? Our families came together to discuss what the funeral would look like.

What flowers? What songs? Who would speak?

I didn't know.

Then, the dreaded question: "What did your husband want – burial or cremation?"

My husband was twenty-four years old when he was taken from us.

Who makes funeral plans or considers whether they want to be buried or cremated at the age of twenty-four?

Seriously, who thinks they're going to die at twenty-four?

"Put him in Tupperware. He'll last forever."

I don't know if nerves caused my mouth to open and blurt this out, but there it was. My husband used to say it to me as a joke, and now I'd put it out there.

I couldn't help it. It was sort of funny, and maybe it was what I needed to cope with everything.

There was a stony silence.

Not everyone thought the way I did.

I wanted to explain that he used to say that because his mother was a Tupperware consultant. But I didn't. We just pushed on with the preparations.

My husband had been a public patient but, owing to the accident, he was classed as a third-party insurance patient. There was to be a court case.

Until you are in this situation yourself, you can't possibly be aware of what is involved. I was stunned. Every tissue, every swab – everything was accounted for and claimed by the public system through a claims case that dragged out over eight long years. The court system is agonising. I didn't understand why it had to take so long. My husband was dead; you can't get any better or any worse when you're dead. At the time, the long delay was explained to me as being because the insurance company were waiting to see if I remarried.

I didn't remarry.

On the day I had to be in court eight years later, my barrister told me, "Don't look too sexy. A lot will depend on whether the judge has had sex recently and what mood he's in."

I was astounded. What did the way I looked and dressed have to do with anything? My husband had died. I'd been left to pick up the pieces with two small children.

As time progressed, I came to know more about what actually happened that night. My husband was riding pillion. As they approached the corner, the owner of the bike lost control and hit the gutter. The impact catapulted my husband to the end of the vacant block. He came down on his head and slid to the back of the block where he landed under the back fence. The driver stayed in hospital overnight. He went home the next day. I've never heard from him, although I suppose he's been living with the memory of that night ever since, as my children and I also live with the outcome.

Witnesses were flown in from all around the country to testify. All of us sat in the halls of the Supreme Court for most of the day while both sides argued the case. Eventually, they reached a settlement. Nobody was called to testify and everyone was sent home. A colossal waste of time.

Reflection 1

More people need to see the bigger picture of the devastation left behind after a split-second decision. One life can impact so many others.

We all have something we would have, on reflection, done differently.

Would I go through this experience all over again?

No.

Do I appreciate where it has brought me?

Yes.

We must appreciate life and the time we have on this planet. We must live each day as if it is our last. I'm not suggesting you go out and spend all your money or jump out of planes. I'm suggesting you decide on a life you would love to live and take steps to create that life by design. Don't be the person who gets to the end of their life saying, "I wish I did …"

We all deserve better than that.

Is fear holding you back from achieving your dreams? Start to notice thoughts and feelings that paralyse you. Face those fears. Make fear your friend. Write your fear down and notice what comes up for you. Don't dismiss what your body and thoughts are trying to tell you, because these are the first steps towards being consciously aware.

The secret of change is to focus all of your energy not on fighting the old, but on building the new.

~ Socrates ~

CHAPTER TWO:
The Merry-Go-Round

Widowed with a two-year-old and about to have our second child, I was terrified. Fear of the unknown consumed me. I fought my doubts every day – a never-ending internal battle – but what choice did I have? I had to survive as there was no-one else to look after my children. Natural instinct eventually kicked in and I started taking each day as it came, keeping my focus on my children. I stayed busy – perhaps too busy – so I didn't have to deal with the loss and grief.

Without an education, the only thing I could do was go on the sole parent pension. It's not a place I dreamed I'd ever be, but there you are! It's not exactly something you plan on, having the government take care of your family. I certainly didn't have a plan now, either; I just existed because that's what I'd always done.

One thing I was becoming increasingly concerned about was the sex of my baby. I desperately wanted a boy because another girl would mean there would be no child to carry on my husband's name.

Finally, I arranged an ultrasound.

"It's a boy," the sonographer said.

I was so relieved. In my mind, it was like my husband being reborn in my son. I needed to believe this to come to some kind of acceptance about what had happened. There must have been something in it because years later, when I was looking at my husband's childhood class photo and my son's class photo from when he was around the same age, I would have sworn it was the same person. It brought me a sense of peace.

The maternity staff at the hospital also had some concerns about the effects of the ongoing stress on me and my unborn son. When I went into labour they put me on a syntocinon drip; however, it was still a long and hard birth. All I recall afterwards is sleeping and sleeping; the hospital staff were very understanding and supportive.

Sleep really was the only way my system could cope with everything that had happened. I'd moved up a level – I was now a widow with a two-year-old and a newborn. I had no idea if I was strong enough to do this on my own.

What I soon came to realise, however, is that I'm a fighter. I became a fighter through this experience and, still to this day, I have a determination in me to recognise my fears and fight them before they consume me. My children needed me.

Unfortunately, despite this realisation, I fell straight into what was comfortable.

Reflection 2

My father was a 'Clayton's father' – he was there but he wasn't. I had a dad but I didn't. My two children had a dad but they didn't, though not for the same reasons. I had to be both Mum and Dad to my kids.

It was so important for me to do things differently from what I was born into. I desperately wanted to be there for my children – to love them and do things with them. I wanted them to have more than what I had.

To a point I achieved this, but those learned behaviours are so ingrained that you are not even aware they are a part of your make-up.

As much as I did do things differently from the parenting I'd received, those patterns were always there – deep down. Behaviours and ways of thinking that were so ingrained I wasn't aware they were part of who I was. They were my go-to because I didn't know anything else. Learned behaviours from watching what my parents did; behaviours my parents learned from watching what their parents did.

We all carry imprints that impact our choices in every area of our lives. The interactions I had and those I witnessed have impacted me most of my life.

Do you recognise situations connected to your childhood that have influenced or moulded your outcomes?
Sit with this question. Don't be quick to dismiss it.
This is a powerful insight.
Be still and listen to that small voice inside of you.

*My life and my journey do not
have to define my outcomes.*

CHAPTER THREE:
Growing up in a Dysfunctional Environment

Where do I begin?

My 'wild ride' started when I first came into this world, born into a family who had already set the course of what was to come.

I was always different. The kid who just didn't quite fit in. Today, I know I don't have to fit in. I accept me as the unique person I am. However, as a young person I didn't know that so I spent most of my life trying to be accepted. The thing was, in doing so I accepted the unacceptable, yet was not accepted myself – despite my attempts to mould myself into anything others wanted me to be.

I was alone in a family of six.

Dad was either working or drunk. Mum was working, and when she wasn't she couldn't be a mum because she was always stressed due to Dad's drinking. My two much older sisters were off, doing their thing. That left me and my younger sister – and we continually locked horns.

The baby of the family is often the one who gets mollycoddled. My family was no different in that respect. It didn't matter what happened between the two of us, I was always the one blamed for upsetting the baby. I couldn't win! It didn't matter what I said; she was right and I was wrong.

I learned to avoid unnecessary interactions. Even when I was very sick I'd still go to school – it was better than being home alone with my sister because, ultimately, we'd end up fighting. I'd be in the wrong, of course. Feeling awful at school was the better alternative – and that's saying something, because school wasn't my safe space either. It was difficult.

In my mind, my only option was to keep everyone at a distance and become invisible. If you're invisible, you can't be blamed for anything. If you were a good girl and kept your head low, you wouldn't get in trouble.

Who was I kidding?

If I died and fell over, someone would tell me I'd fallen the wrong way. That's how I felt; that's just the way it was.

My imprints started at a very early age.

Life in a violent alcoholic family was my normal. I'm not saying it was easy but I didn't know anything else.

Every day was like walking a well-worn road. I knew every turn. Knew what was around the corner. I didn't like what was coming but I didn't know there was anything different. It was normal – whatever normal means.

Mum and Dad would leave early for work each day, so it was up to us kids to get ourselves ready and off to school. We were never in the same house for long due to Dad's alcoholism. Moving house meant moving schools. That's hard on anyone, let alone a child who wasn't confident at the best of times.

When I was in Year 3, I had friends at school. It was the first time I'd ever had friends. Then we moved. I lost the only friends I knew. After that, I decided I wasn't going to change schools again. Instead, I rode my bike five kilometres to school and back every day. It was too late, though. The damage was done. I didn't know how to connect with people; it was easier to isolate myself and pretend I didn't care.

At the age of thirteen, I had a knee operation and was on crutches for weeks afterwards. My parents were so caught up in their own stuff I had no choice but to hobble to school and back every day – a ten-kilometre round trip – with my bag swinging precariously from my shoulder.

That was my family. Everyone on their own; everyone fending for themselves. My home life was a huge secret. Nobody would believe me if I spoke up, and I didn't want to get my parents in trouble. Nor did I want to cop it from them.

It was much safer to say nothing at all.

It was much safer to continue doing what I'd been doing for years and just wait and hope for things to improve.

The only person I could rely on was me.

I had no friends.

My parents didn't have friends either; none who they'd invite over to our house, anyway. There was the occasional relative who'd come and visit. It never ended well. Everyone would be on the booze and it would end in a big argument.

Dad's day would often start with a 'largie' rather than breakfast. "A beer is like having steak and eggs," he'd say if anyone questioned him.

Drinking interfered with everything in our lives. Things would just blow up on a daily basis. We all walked around like the floor was made of eggshells. None of us wanted to be the person who set him off again. I learned from a young age how to stay out of the firing line. I'd go to my room and shut the door, hoping it would be over soon.

Dad's drinking was all-consuming for Mum and us kids. We thought of little else. There was no room in our thinking to consider school or friends. We couldn't bring friends home because we never knew what state he'd be in. Everything revolved around Dad and his precious XXXX.

In our house, Dad was king. Everyone lived in fear of his moods; we could only hope we were doing the right thing. The claws of alcoholism were deeply rooted in our behaviours and reactions. That was the way it was.

My sister and I saw Dad's drinking as an opportunity to get some pocket money. He stacked all his largies under the house, between the concrete piers. We knew that when the stack got to a certain height, which didn't take that long, we could fill the boot of the car and go and cash them in at the bottle shop.

Amber liquid ran through his veins. I don't recall him ever being sober. He'd fall asleep on the toilet and Mum would put a mattress in the doorway so he wouldn't get hurt if he fell. There was only one toilet, so the rest of us had to use a bucket.

Every afternoon, if Dad wasn't at home, we knew where he was – the hotel. When it got late, Mum piled us all in the car and off we'd go to pick him up. As Mum drove in stony silence, we sat, quiet and still, sliding out hands slowly down behind the seats, feeling for coins; pocket money to spend.

We had a very important role to play once we arrived at the hotel. We knew the drill. Go and fetch Dad.

On the one hand, it was exciting because Dad would sit us up at the bar and buy us all a 'double sars'. We loved that drink – it was fizzy sarsaparilla with a shot of sarsaparilla cordial. For us, getting this drink was as good as Christmas coming early.

On the other hand, we knew Mum was sitting in the car, waiting for all of us to come out with Dad.

Waiting, waiting, waiting. Her temperature rising like a thermometer on a hot day. We knew what was coming. We knew the thermometer would explode at some point that night.

Dad came out to the car when he was good and ready. Never before. He didn't care. He wasn't worried about the thermometer.

Once we got home, it would be on for young and old. No holds barred. It would usually become physical. Us kids scattered like ants do when you pour a drop of water in their nest. We'd all go to our safe spots – for me, it was my bedroom. We'd listen to the fight, the yells, the thumps. Mum always came off second best.

There was crazy stuff, too. The type of things parents don't do – not that we knew that at the time.

During the floods, he piled Mum, me and my sister into a truck and drove to work because he forgot to put a lock on a pump. The water was up to the top of the truck tyres. The road was dirt, with little timber bridges we had to cross; we couldn't see the road, though. My sister and I were screaming because the water kept getting deeper. The road was so narrow, we wondered how he'd turn the truck around. It was terrifying, but all Dad was worried about was getting the lock on the pump. Somehow, he eventually turned the truck around and we went back home.

He'd often be hungry after he'd spent the afternoon drinking at the hotel and was always rummaging around in the kitchen, looking for food. One night, he nearly burned the house down because he'd put a pan on the stove with some oil to cook some chips but fell asleep. Luckily, Mum woke up and got us all out of the house. It did a lot of damage to the kitchen so we had to move again.

One morning, we woke up to find the car covered with mud and reeds. We never found out what happened or how the car got in such a state.

These types of things were not unusual in our family. We didn't bring friends home because we never knew what they would walk in on. Best to keep people at a distance so they didn't ask.

How my father didn't kill himself or someone else I don't know. He lost control of a semitrailer and went over a cliff when I was very little. At work one time, he was cold so he made a fire and threw petrol on it. People protected him – Mum, his boss – nobody else could believe he did stupid stuff like that.

But we believed it.

It was our normal.

The drinking got worse as the years went on.

One time, Dad had blood coming out the pores of his skin and the doctor was called. "If you don't stop drinking," the doctor said, "you'll be dead in six months."

After the doctor left, Mum and my older sisters immediately started pouring his beer down the sink.

It made no difference. He just got more.

Not even the fear of death could make Dad stop drinking. "I'll outlive you all," he'd say. He was like a cat with more than nine lives.

Dad's drinking and his violence against Mum impacted her life. There are only so many times you can tolerate having your head smashed into a wall or going into the hospital and lying about why you needed stitches.

She tried suiciding.

We were standing there, watching as Dad and our neighbour wrestled with her as they tried to get her into the car. She was kicking and screaming, her arms and legs going everywhere. We were also standing there while Mum had her stomach pumped. All I remember is that she had this really big stomach full of water.

What sort of impact does that have on a child?

Mum ended up in the psychiatric ward. Visiting her was scary. Her ward was full of really strange people, all talking to themselves. Mum was there – but it wasn't Mum. Our highlight ended up being playing cricket with the male staff.

When she came out of hospital, Mum had obviously decided 'if you can't beat them, then why not join them?'

Now we had Mum drinking, as well as Dad.

Reflection 3

My childhood was an existence only and my childhood fears ran deep. One of these fears was about being seen as unnecessary; having no worth.

Fears often begin with the smallest of events. In my case, I came home from school every day and did my chores. One day, I decided to mop the floor. I wanted to help my mum and I truly believed I was. Except, Mum came home from work and mopped the floor again. I didn't say anything. She didn't know I'd mopped the floor. I felt sad and useless. It was such a small thing but it impacted me very deeply as a young person.

My limiting belief was 'I am not good enough'. I told myself Mum had to mop the floor again because I hadn't done a good enough job. Why should I even bother trying?

This belief fed into every aspect of my life, including school. I took the easy road and got what I always got – nothing. The same result, every time.

The perceptions I developed during my childhood – the beliefs of my smaller self – impacted my life moving forward. Until I cleared these beliefs, change would not happen for me.

The environment I grew up in didn't support independent thinking or self-esteem. As a child, I lived every day in fear; my world was full of violence. As my mother prepared the evening meal, her mind was on my father. How the evening unfolded was dependent on when he arrived home. If he was late, things would get ugly, scattering all of us kids to our bedrooms until it was over. My mother usually came off worse, with a black eye or the need for stitches. It was 'normal'.

As a child, I only knew what I knew, which was not a lot. Today, I've become someone who is open and willing to continue learning who she is as a person.

Life is a journey that will only come to an end when I die.

Have you had childhood experiences that continue to impact your life today?

I did; that is why it is so important for me to make the decision to deal with those things that rise up and not dismiss them. They let me know there is something I need to address in me. What do you need to address in you?

Nobody can impose your beliefs on you.
It's always you who in the last instance can
permit a belief to be true for you or not.
~ Marc Reklau ~

CHAPTER FOUR:
School – the First Time Round

School was little more than a curse.

I was isolated because of my circumstances. My family had moved every time there was an 'incident' – like whenever the arguing spilled out onto the street for the world to see and hear. I had no childhood friends – what was the point when we'd have to move again soon anyway? The older you get, the harder it is to go up to someone at school and say hello; the harder it is to fit in.

Each time we moved I went further inside myself. It was safer than showing I was hurting or scared. As a child, it was easier to be invisible and stay in the background.

There was no-one to teach us how to communicate, and nobody recognised where we were both coming from. It was always my fault, no matter what. I hated being blamed for every feeling and emotion that my sister had. Mum wouldn't take the time to find out. The same thing happened at school – teachers would come to their own conclusions. The majority of the time, they were wrong. It was so much easier to be as far away from my sister as possible. It was the easy road.

My younger sister and I couldn't even do the dishes at the same time because it would always end up in another argument. I desperately wanted an escape from it all. Being at a different school gave that to me for a period of time. Ultimately, though, I had to go home at the end of the day. It was something I learned to live with.

I don't do this today. I know I will get so much further by facing myself and what is going on inside of me that I will make the most gain for my growth. These days, I show my grandchildren how we all come at things from a different perspective. I love it when I can work through situations with them and they say, "It was nobody's fault," and apologise to each other because they are open and willing to see the other's perspective.

The fear – those feelings and emotions that keep me going back to what's comfortable – never really went away. For a long time, I only knew what I'd watched my parents do. When fear rose up, I'd go straight back to what I knew because that kept me safe. It also kept me from moving forward into the best version of myself. It's like a dog chasing its tail. That's what I did for such a long time. I had no destination in mind, only a need to survive.

Not every class at school was awful. I loved my business studies subject. I loved it because I was good at it. It was something I understood and enjoyed. When I think about it, I was accepted in that class too. The teacher encouraged me, and I felt good that I was achieving something in my life. I could have gone a long way if I'd stuck it out but it was only a small portion of the rest of my school life and, at the end of the day, it wasn't enough for me to see it through and stay at school. Those deep-rooted limiting beliefs that have always held me back also stopped me from doing something I loved.

The only thing that kept me going a lot of the time was the prize – graduating high school.

Except, I ended up not getting the prize.

It was a decision I made, failing myself when I was at school. I took the easy road and gave up.

I was sick of feeling dumb in front of my peers because I couldn't answer the teachers' questions. They didn't understand my mind was elsewhere: 'What do I have to do after school? Peel the beans and peas. Make sure everything is just right. Hope the yelling, screaming and fighting wouldn't happen that night.'

Nobody could understand my normal, and I didn't have the words or the desire to explain it to anyone. I believed it was better to fly under the radar. All I wanted to do was sink into the background and not be seen. My homelife was a subject that stayed hidden. The teachers didn't know. My peers didn't know. That worked for me.

With the exception of business studies, I didn't enjoy any of my subjects. One of the worst was sex education. Most of the time I just sat there while the teacher droned on, but then there was the homework. One time, we were supposed to do a report on one of the topics.

What did I know about sex?

Nobody talked about it at home. I'd never been given the 'talk' when I went through puberty. No help. I never asked questions either; all of my focus was on getting my chores done so Mum and Dad didn't get into an argument.

All I knew about sex was that it involved Mum yelling at Dad to get on his own side of the bed.

I was so far out of my comfort zone with this report, it wasn't funny.

The other subject I really dreaded was maths. I just didn't understand it. Crunch-time, and the cherry on top of my whole school experience, came when my maths teacher put a spotlight on me.

"So," she said, "perhaps you'd like to share your process and your answer with the class?"

I physically shrank down into my chair, sliding down and hunching my shoulders over to make myself appear as small as I felt.

I didn't have any answer, let alone the right one. I knew that. The teacher also knew that, yet she'd still asked me.

I sat there, staring at a spot on my desk, like the proverbial stunned mullet.

The other students laughed. I had no idea what to do or say. All I wanted was to disappear.

Dumb. That's how I felt all the time, but right at that moment I'd never felt more stupid. The teacher offered no guidance. No support.

"Clearly you don't know," she said and then moved her attention to someone else.

I'm sure she had no idea how she made me feel that day. It was the worst thing that could have happened to me at that point in my life. Worse than the fights at home. Worse than not feeling loved.

I felt worthless. I felt stupid.

I'd had enough.

I quit.

I just couldn't face school anymore.

I took the first job that came along. It was clothes sorting. Why not? It was a job. I was earning my own money; how good was that! It had to be better than feeling worthless and stupid – didn't it? Besides, I wasn't capable of doing anything else. I wasn't smart enough. I certainly didn't deserve anything better.

That limited thinking held me back from achieving and succeeding for years.

I bumped into my business teacher one day at the shopping centre, not long after I'd left school. We chatted very briefly, just trivial stuff. She turned to go, then looked back at me at the last minute. "You had so much potential to go a long way in business," she said.

I didn't have a response for that. Did she know something I didn't? Even if I'd pursued a career in business, would I have only failed myself with my self-doubt? What would I have done if someone questioned me? Would I have walked away because I didn't have the self-confidence to believe in myself or the self-esteem to see it through? This is how powerful those childhood imprints were for me.

Today, I don't sit and ponder what life could have been because my journey has brought me to the place I'm meant to be now. All the lessons have helped to create the person I am today. I embrace opportunities. I come at life from a totally different perspective.

What do I want? That's the question I ask myself today.

Reflection 4

In my early adult life I hated moving. I needed stability. My background dictated that staying in the one place was extremely important. But I have grown past this perspective. Home to me now is where I lay my head. I am comfortable in my own skin today. If I wish to move or do something differently, that's okay. I'm no longer standing in the shadows of what other people expect of me. I'm an individual and a human being that can make my own decisions and follow through with them if I so desire.

It's taken me a long time to work through all the things I've been through, but I reflect on everything. I now believe that everything in my life happened for a reason. Everything in my past life has brought me to the life I'm living now.

I'm very grateful for my journey.

I'm also grateful I can support others and bring so much to the people I help. I've walked the journey. I've been there and come through the other side with more awareness and gratitude.

I listen to my inner voice more today than I ever have. Though it's still small, that voice is my companion and we walk this road together without fear we'll get it wrong.

Wrong is only a word. It does not define me.

Anything is possible when you dream it so. I would never have believed the life I'm living today was possible, but here I am living my dream and using my passion to support others. I couldn't be doing that if I didn't first do it for myself.

Life is what I want to make it.
This is my life. What about your life? What do you want for your life? If you could create a life you would love, what would that life look like?
I ask myself these questions every day.

When we treat people merely as they are, they will remain as they are. When we treat them as if they were what they should be, they will become what they should be.
~ Thomas S Monson ~

CHAPTER FIVE:
Familiar Paths – Again and Again

The inner voice that pulls you to what is familiar and comfortable runs deep.

My younger sister and I used to have full-on fights. She had long fingernails that she used to gouge chunks of skin out of my arms. I'd grab hold of her hair and pull till it came out. The fights were always real doozies; very unpleasant.

"You hate me," she'd scream at me.

"No, I love you," I always replied. "That's why we fight."

How mixed up is this statement?

This was the life I was living. The way our parents interacted was all we knew and all we had to go by. Our parents fought like this every night. It was their normal. It was our normal.

All I knew was that fighting meant relationships, love and respect.

My bedroom was my safe place at home. I found comfort there when there was commotion everywhere else. I built a fantasy world where I dreamed of my own Prince Charming coming to save me. I planned for the day we'd ride off into the sunset and live happily ever after.

Who was I kidding?

It was nothing more than a Cinderella fantasy, but I held onto it for a long time. I needed that dream. Then, one day, it seemed to come true.

There was a boy two doors down the road from our house. I found him 'interesting'.

He came from the same type of family as I did but I didn't recognise that. Looking back, I'm not sure I was aware exactly what my attraction to him was at first. Did I want to save him? Or was he my Prince Charming, sent to save me from the family I was born into?

It soon became apparent that he'd come into my life as my saviour. Or at least, that's how I saw it.

I loved him with all my heart.

My family, however, didn't.

At first they had no idea he was even on the scene. I'd kept it a secret – it was like a game. He was older than me and, I suppose, more experienced in life. Even if he wasn't older, my parents would've thought I was too young anyway.

As a teenager you don't want to listen to your parents. What would they know?

I was a virgin, and he talked me into to having sex with him even though I was underage. As usual, I didn't make the decision for myself. I wanted him to like me, so I said yes. I can't say it was a wonderful experience. I didn't respect myself at all afterwards because I'd allowed another person to manipulate me.

I would have done anything for this boy, though. I loved him. At least, I thought I did.

I'd been seeing a counsellor for a while after things had suddenly become impossible at home. At first, it was awkward – no fifteen-year-old wants to blurt their soul out to an adult.

"Everything you say will stay within these walls," she told me at our first meeting. "Our conversations are confidential."

I quickly started trusting this counsellor but, more than that, I needed someone to talk to. So, one day, I spilled out my heart. I spoke openly and even told her about my boyfriend who was older than me.

She betrayed my trust and told my parents about my boyfriend. About the sex.

My parents were furious and there was a huge argument. They wanted to charge him with 'carnal knowledge'. I begged them not to and that's when they sent me to live with my sister. She lived an hour away, and I knew they hoped the distance would end the relationship.

It didn't.

One night, my sister was out and I was left to babysit. After a while, I heard a noise outside. It honestly sounded like someone trying to break in. I was terrified. There was nobody to help. In desperation, I called my boyfriend. He came over on his motorbike.

"You just made that up," my sister said when she got home. "You were just looking for an excuse to see him."

I wasn't making it up but nobody believed me. The experience left me unable to live in ground-level housing for years.

Eventually I moved back home. It wasn't working with my sister and I was too far from school. My parents tried to lay down some ground rules, but by that stage I didn't care.

The minute they found out we were still very much 'together' they clamped down on what I was allowed to do, trying to make things even harder than they already were.

"He's a bad influence," my mother said – again and again.

Boundaries were set and rules were made and enforced. They had enough sense not to ban me from seeing him, but they did ban him from setting foot on our property. If we were going out, he wasn't allowed to come and pick me up at the door.

Being teenagers, we worked around it. Getting out of the house wasn't usually a problem because Dad would either be at work or the pub. If not, he'd be passed out somewhere in our backyard or the toilet, or he'd be balancing on the chair at the dining table. Mum would be preoccupied with Dad and his drinking – or with her own drinking by this time.

We arranged that I'd sit on the back doorstep when I was ready. He'd come out the back of his house and then we'd both leave and meet out the front on the footpath. Usually it worked, but if my parents spotted him, which sometimes happened, there'd be a huge blow-up. Abusive language and yelling could be heard all the way down the street. It was so embarrassing, but that was my life – a constant cycle of arguing or silence.

Whenever the arguing between Mum and Dad started, my boyfriend – being only two houses away – would hear. He'd come and lay on the footpath outside our house, listening. "If I need to rescue you, at least I'll be close," he told me.

I imagined him charging in on his white stallion, sweeping me up and carrying me away. 'He must love me so much,' I thought.

Then, one night, my parents were arguing as usual and our dog started barking. Dad went rushing out of the house, yelling at the dog to shut up, and spotted my boyfriend on the footpath. It was on for young and old. Fists were flying everywhere. Mum and I were screaming. The next minute my boyfriend's mother came running up the street, and suddenly her and Mum are in a fist fight of their own. I can still see these four grown adults in this big punch-up, yelling and screaming at each other, with me around the edges trying to stop it. None of this was even close to normal. But, still, it was all I knew.

It seemed to go on for a long time, but it may have only been minutes because the police weren't called by the neighbours.

"You need to get out," my boyfriend said to me not long after. He was very convincing and I really didn't know any better. "Move in with us."

So, I did as I was told. I left home and moved in with his family. I was still only fifteen and legally not supposed to be moving out without my parents' permission, but they couldn't say anything because I had the backing of a psychologist my boyfriend had taken me to see. She arranged it all.

The day I left, my sisters went through my things and took what they wanted from my stuff.

I was an outcast after that – if I wasn't already one. I'd never felt like I belonged.

Him, on the other hand, I trusted completely. As far as I was concerned, I was doing the right thing. He loved me – I truly believe that. However, I soon learned his family did the same crazy things my family did. One night, his mother threw a beer glass at him. It flew like a bullet and left a perfectly round hole in the window.

Another time, his mother called the police on him and stated that he'd stolen her lawnmower. He'd asked if he could borrow it to do a job. She also threw his possessions out of the house whenever they had a big argument. She'd literally chuck the lot out – all his things, including his clothes and his stereo.

She'd even led him to believe that his father was in jail for raping someone, which was another lie.

These people will do whatever they have to do to keep you in the dysfunctional cycle of alcoholism. Fear keeps you stuck.

I'd left home for this?

I lived at his mother's place for maybe a month before moving into a flat with my boyfriend's sister. That only lasted a couple of weeks – she disappeared. She ran off with her boyfriend and left me on my own in the flat.

"Well," my boyfriend said when I told him she was gone. "You can't live here by yourself." He shook his head. "You can't trust the guys next door."

So, he packed his stuff and moved in with me.

That was that. He didn't ask what I wanted. I never had a voice. I never spoke up. I just accepted that everyone else knew what was best for me. Don't rock the boat – it's the safest way forward.

Anyway, he loved me. Plus, I was so intent on getting out and had no idea I was perpetuating the cycle all over again.

We lived together in the flat for a couple of years before moving to Sydney.

I was a housewife from the age of fifteen.

Reflection 5

At no point in my life had I made any decisions for myself. It had always been my parents, my teachers and now my boyfriend – they were the decision-makers in my life. I just did what I was told, and when.

I was always hoping someone – my Prince Charming – would save me from my life. I was looking for love anywhere and in any form I could find it. I thought love meant giving your all, giving yourself away. The thing is, you must first love yourself before you can truly love someone else.

These days I find it rather funny, those dreams and fantasies I had, because I know it could have been quite different yet I find myself so grateful to have learned those lessons. Grateful for my life because it brought me to where I am today.

Are there times in your life when others made decisions for you, or you hold your tongue because of the backlash you'd get if you voiced your opinion?

Love for self is paramount. I didn't understand this concept back then, and that is why I continued to disrespect myself. Don't allow someone else to disrespect you. Most importantly, don't disrespect yourself.

You are worthy of respect and love.

If you don't love who you are now, then create a vision of who you would love to become. That is the first step of creating the life you would love.

Some people believe holding on and hanging in
there are signs of great strength. However, there
are times when it takes much more strength
to know when to let go and then do it.
~ Ann Landers ~

CHAPTER SIX:
Hard-Knock Lessons

Our move to Sydney was for a business opportunity that ultimately didn't come off as my boyfriend expected. In fact, not only did it not come off, but it was a complete fizzer.

Naturally, I assumed we'd go back to Brisbane. But no, he didn't want to. The people who'd offered the original partnership had asked him to do labouring on their property. He was keen to give it a go and I just went along with it.

No voice. He didn't ask what I thought, anyway.

Then he met this woman at the local shop. One thing led to another. He had it all worked out. When this woman called my boyfriend, the young uni students on the level below us would come and fetch him. He wasn't exactly discreet because the property owners became aware of what was going on. "We've told him to come clean with you," they said.

He didn't.

I was so naïve. I'd had no idea what was going on. Or maybe I knew but didn't want to accept it.

This whole time I was playing along, being the dutiful partner. I worked. I did the cooking and cleaning.

My moment of courage came when I found out I was pregnant and decided I wanted to go home.

"I'm going back to Brisbane," I said. "With you or without you."

It was an ultimatum, though I'm not sure what I would've done if he'd said no.

He decided to go back to Brisbane with me.

On the day we left Sydney, one of our young neighbours pulled me aside. "He doesn't deserve you," she said.

I shrugged. I had no self-respect. It was totally unthinkable to say the words, 'No, I deserve better.' I accepted his behaviour as my lot and truly believed I was lucky to have him.

Even after we got back to Brisbane, he wouldn't let the woman in Sydney go. I sat there listening to his intimate conversations with this woman. All I wanted was to be loved and accepted by this man, and I was willing to put myself in degrading situations to achieve it.

Eventually she ended it. Not that he came back to me – he'd gotten a taste for affairs and just went looking for the next one.

I couldn't let go. I loved him, and what was I going to do if I left? Go back to my dysfunctional family? That wasn't an option for me. So, I stayed and did the best I could with what I had. I did what was expected of me – no matter how bad it got.

This is what my mother did.

I just continued to do what I had always done and got what I always got. The same.

I wasn't taught to respect myself, so how could I put respect into my life?

You only know what you know, good or bad.

Then his mother weighed in on the situation. "You have to get married," she said.

Perhaps it was because she knew about the affairs, but I don't think so. I'm pretty sure it was all about the image. It wouldn't do to have a child out of wedlock.

His mother arranged a meeting with the minister. I got the impression he felt we shouldn't get married, but it was expected and I didn't have the confidence or the education to say I could do this on my own.

My husband-to-be loved his children but he didn't love me. I knew that. What attracted him to me at first was my need, in his eyes, to be saved. That's the way he operated; he wanted to be a saviour. The first affair he had was with a woman who was engaged but not happy in the relationship. He felt he could save her. He only decided to come back to me because I was pregnant with his child. He didn't have a father around when he was growing up and he didn't want his child to not know him.

That's nice, but when you're in a loveless marriage what are you teaching your children? Disrespect. We'd be teaching our future children that disrespect was normal. He didn't respect me and I didn't respect myself. That's what our children would see. Unfortunately, we didn't realise that.

Marriage was a good option for me because I truly believed things would be better when we were a married couple.

They weren't.

He continued to treat me with total disregard and disrespect and, in fact, his behaviours escalated – both physically and emotionally.

I continued to believe in him. I continued to love him. This was my lot and I expected nothing else. However, as time went on, loving him and supporting him became increasingly difficult. We didn't have a relationship – not in the true sense of what a relationship should be.

It was all about my comfort zone and my normal.

I had the baby after we were married. A little girl. He doted on her. But not on me. Still, I stayed. I became pregnant again.

My mother stayed with my father, so of course I must stay and tolerate the unacceptable because that's what a loving wife does. He loved his daughter and he would love our new baby. What right did I have to take that away from him?

Life went on.

Then … the accident happened.

I fought for him. For three months, I fought.

Why?

It was expected. I was his wife. He was the father of my children. Besides, what sort of person would ditch their partner under these circumstances?

In hindsight, though, the reason was deeper – those learned behaviours from my upbringing and what I'd watched and heard in my home with my own parents. It all set the course for this situation and others that followed.

You can't change what you don't know.

If I had that time again, though, I'd know.

He didn't deserve me.

At some point in those terrible months, something clicked. Maybe it started with the driving licence? Whatever it was, I thought I was ready to make changes and alter my journey to move towards becoming someone totally different to what I was born into.

Yes, it was for my children. Ultimately though, it was for me.

Reflection 6

There was no respect for me in any of this – not from others and certainly not from myself. I thought my handsome prince had saved me but all I was doing was following in my mother's footsteps. I didn't have the foresight or the understanding to realise my happy ever after wasn't going to happen.

I didn't know I could expect respect, and I didn't know how to respect myself because respect was not part of my upbringing. You cannot learn or develop skills without good role models or knowledge.

When you have lived most of your life doing what other people expect, you lose yourself. That's what happened to me. I didn't know how to make decisions for myself. If I did make a decision, I had no idea how to follow through on it. When I tried to follow through I'd get scared; the fear would keep rising until I went back to what was comfortable and known.

My brain would say, 'You don't know the outcome of that choice because it's not guaranteed. Because it's not guaranteed, you'd better stay with what you know.'

Before my first husband died, I only existed.

I thought I needed him because without him I was nothing.

My fantasy of happily ever after was so twisted. Yes, he saved me and got me out of my terrible situation, but I'm not certain whether I moved from worse to better, better to worse, or just stayed on the same playing field but with different players.

The thing is, I know there's no point saying, 'What if …?'

I can't change my story.

I don't want to change my story.

> **Knowledge is power.**
> *When you consider your behaviours or reactions to something, have you heard yourself say, "I know where that comes from"? Do you really know where it comes from? Do you really know what is truly happening in your life? If you do know, are you ready to embrace that knowledge? Are you ready to say 'yes' for yourself? Are you ready to learn and to grow and to explore your imprints?*

---

*Don't lose your dignity and self-respect trying
to make people accept, love and appreciate
you when they just aren't capable.*
- Attitude to Inspiration -

CHAPTER SEVEN:
Barely Contained

Quite some time after the death of my husband, the son of one of his workmates started popping in occasionally to help out around the house. I appreciated it because there were things to be done that I just didn't have the skills or, with the kids, the time to do.

The occasional visits became regular ones.

After a while, he just moved in.

There wasn't a discussion. No decision was made. It just happened. And I went along with it, never thinking to question whether it was something I truly wanted. I just accepted it. It wasn't until after he moved in that I realised what he was truly like – an alcoholic, and a violent one – and by then it was too late.

Life with my first husband was difficult. However, those difficulties increased tenfold with my new partner. I was scared before, but now the fear was even worse due to the violence and the unwanted sex. This became my new normal.

"Stay on your side of the bed." My mother's voice echoed in my ears as my partner forced himself on me and I found myself repeating those words. Learned behaviours from my childhood playing out in my adult life.

I'd grown up in a violent, alcoholic environment. It defined my life. It was my normal. I was completely under his control. Once again I was walking on eggshells, waiting for things to explode. Thinking 'if I'm a good girl, if I do what I'm told, it will be okay', but knowing it wouldn't be okay. No room for chitchat with the kids. No 'How was your day?' or 'What did you do at school?' My mind was on my alcoholic partner, just like Mum's mind had been on Dad. Doing my chores, having the meat and three veg ready, making sure everything was in order and hoping – praying – we could have a lovely evening. That hope shattered every time.

The cycle of abuse and apology was never-ending. Unfulfilled promises – I'd heard them all with Dad and now I was hearing the same ones as an adult. Always believing them, the same as Mum had. I went with the flow. It was normal.

All the 'antics' that happened with Dad were being replicated in my adult life with my partner. Drinking before going out, drinking at the event and then polishing off any leftover alcohol back at home. Running into a glass door because he didn't see it. Falling asleep on the toilet. Leaning on me as I tried to drag him upstairs and into bed.

All the time I protected him, did everything I could to stop him hurting himself – the same way Mum did with Dad. Never once did it cross my mind that it might have been better to let him fall, to let him get hurt, because then he may have asked for help.

Why would I think to do that, though?

I truly believed it was my duty to protect him and that he would eventually realise what was happening. I told myself that if I loved him enough and did everything he needed he would love me and think I was wonderful.

Getting involved with this man just happened. Staying involved was easier than breaking away.

I obeyed.

I lived in fear.

I hid it from the outside world.

Not every day was awful. While he was sober, he was lovely. When he picked up a drink, however, he became very nasty – angry and violent. I was frightened and couldn't see a way out. If he said jump, I jumped.

I owned my home, I had money in the bank, but I had no control over either.

"Let's put in a pool," he said.

I went along with it.

"My parents want to buy a boat to run a fishing business," he said.

I gave them the money.

I even bought my own engagement ring. How pathetic is that?

I handed over the money time and time again.

Why couldn't I say no?

The fights became worse as time went on. We all lived in fear – me and my children – but I couldn't see any way out.

His jealousy was a huge trigger.

He was jealous of the relationship I had with my kids. He was jealous of my dead husband. If we went to the cemetery, I'd have to wait in the car while he took my children to see where their father was buried. He made the children call him 'Dad'.

He was jealous of other men. He accused me of sleeping with his stepfather. If I looked at another man, he'd shout at me that I was having an affair. The accusations if I so much as said hello to someone – particularly a male – escalated.

"You like him more than me, don't you!" he'd yell.

"No," I'd say, "I love you." It was the only thing I could say, but it made no difference. My interpretation of love was skewed anyway.

I was always trying to stay one step ahead. I didn't want to upset him. But then he'd start an argument, giving himself justification to go to the pub and get drunk. I'd try and pretend I was asleep when I heard him come back but sometimes that didn't work. If he wanted sex he would just force himself on me and have what he wanted. I had to just lay there and pretend I wanted it too. Today, I'd say that was rape. Today, I'd know this was alcoholism and I'd know that when the alcoholic gets help and understands the disease they have they are very remorseful. Back then I didn't understand any of that.

I couldn't even be polite to people in my own home. One of the guys from the football team came over one day and, not wanting to be rude, I spoke to him. There was nothing out of the ordinary said; I just asked about his family and his week. After he left, I copped a blasting. Apparently my polite conversation was a 'come-on'.

Withdrawing from people seemed to be my only option. I started actively avoiding people. If I spotted a neighbour or someone I knew at the supermarket or on the street, I'd automatically turn the other way or cross the road so I didn't have to speak with them. It just wasn't worth the trouble.

This was my world.

"Things would be different if we had a baby," he said to me, over and over. So I went along with that, too.

Nothing changed.

If anything, things got a lot worse.

My son loved cuddles and was always snuggling up to me. My partner didn't seem to like this and started paying out on his little boy. "You're a mummy's boy," he'd say.

His grandfather joined in one afternoon when we were visiting, having travelled down south especially to see him. They'd both been on the booze for a while. "Suck up," they sneered. "Mummy's boy."

After that visit we went camping; a 'holiday'. There was, of course, plenty of booze in the cooler. The nitpicking and teasing started up again, but this time our son ran away.

"I can't find him," I cried, terrified.

I searched and searched for hours. Nothing. Finally, he came back on his own. My partner just sat by the fire, drinking. He said nothing while I explained to my son how scared I was and how someone could have grabbed him.

My son was wounded emotionally by his father. With all the mean comments, they never had a close relationship. My son just listened and didn't say much. We all felt it was safer to just go to bed and hope things would improve in the morning. Of course, everything just got buried and was never spoken about.

Eventually my son stopped coming near me. There were no more cuddles. Our relationship disintegrated, broken by his own father's jealousy.

Can you imagine a little boy living in fear of his father paying out on him again and again if he got close his mother?

Yet even this wasn't enough for me to leave the situation, such was the pull my partner had over me.

I couldn't leave.

Not when things continued to get worse.

Not when the violence increased.

Not when my children stood, screaming, at my bedroom door as I was having the crap beaten out of me.

Why?

Was it fear? Lack of confidence? The inability to see another path?

From my childhood imprints, this situation was normal. My parents fought and argued but they stayed together. I thought that was what love looked like; how it was meant to play out.

How wrong can a person be?

At one point, I went to his mother and showed her the bruising. That's how desperate I was.

Her response? "He's my son and I love him."

What I didn't know at the time was that she had also lived with the same sort of violence. It's a generational problem and deeply rooted. She did eventually decide to leave her husband, and that very day he had a work accident and died. I wonder if she actually would have left. The control these types of people have over people like me is incomprehensible to others who have not experienced this type of fear. It's not that easy to break away from it.

My mother tried to help. She tried to tell me early on that he was an alcoholic. She'd recognised the signs because she had sought help for herself, but I hadn't seen them. My understanding of an alcoholic was someone lying in the gutter or sleeping it off on a park bench. What I didn't understand was that an alcoholic can hold down a job and have a family. They can be 'outside angels' but 'inside devils'. I had no idea I was protecting him and enabling him to do the things he did.

I did actually end it once.

It wasn't long before he was back, full of apologies and promises it would never happen again. I wanted to believe him. I didn't want to be on my own.

What was wrong with me?

Nothing.

I was caught in a cycle.

I was on autopilot.

People around me saw my behaviour well before they saw his – if they ever saw his. I was seen as the crazy, screaming woman. It was the only way I knew how to be heard, though it didn't really have the effect I needed it to have.

Finally, after years of fighting, I realised I was tired.

I stopped fighting back.

Reflection 7

Every time I tried to take back what was mine – to take back my control – fear stopped me. It completely overwhelmed me. I was a doormat to anyone and everyone. It was learned behaviour after years of watching my parents and the way they treated each other.

My childhood experiences impacted me so deeply I couldn't see an alternative way to live my life. Childhood imprints guided my choices as an adult. Looking back, I understand why I accepted it – following the same pathway was a natural progression; there was no need to question it.

If you want respect, you must learn how to love and respect yourself first.

I know that now.

If I could turn back the clock, I know I could make decisions for my benefit. Today I love and respect myself, but I could have learned how to do that much earlier. It's not an easy road by any means, particularly when there are no positive role models, but it is possible.

I will always be grateful to my mum for introducing me to the 12-Step Program. It opened my eyes to what I was living in. Over time, my energy and focus started to change to me. It was me that had the problem. It was me that was reacting to behaviours outside of myself. I started to go within and realise I could have power over my situation, but it wasn't going to happen overnight. I had to get to know me. I didn't understand that concept at the time, but I trusted in the process. I am so glad I did.

> *We all have the right to choose what is best for ourselves, even if others disagree.*
> *Sometimes it is easier to stay, to leave things as they are. But we all deserve better.*
> *What do you truly want for your life? What small changes can you make today?*
> *We all have a choice. It is truly up to us to decide for ourselves. Don't let fear stand in your way.*

Whether you believe you can do a
thing or not, you are right.
~ Henry Ford ~

CHAPTER EIGHT:
Regaining Control of My Circumstances

Strangely enough, it was my mother who opened the door to my escape. I was defaulting to what I knew because it was all I knew, but Mum saw what was happening. Perhaps she saw herself. She couldn't help herself, but she could help me.

"Try this program," she said. "It's a 12-step program for the friends and family of alcoholics."

This was the turning point in my life.

It was my first step towards changing my outcomes.

A little old lady gave me a hug at my first meeting. Her arms wrapped around me and I froze. I was extremely uncomfortable. I'd never had a hug from my parents; that wasn't something we did in our family. I didn't know what to do with this hug. I didn't know how to respond.

What did she want? What was I supposed to do? How was I supposed to act?

I didn't know.

What I did know was that I wanted more. More of what I got that day. More love. More support. More anything. That's why I kept going back.

Even though the whole concept was so foreign it scared me.

Even though I didn't know what I wanted or what I was looking for.

I just knew I wanted to go to the next meeting. And the next. And the next. In fact, I continued going back for over thirty years.

The learning I received over that time was phenomenal. Every meeting, every story I heard, I could take away something that I could use in my situation. I told myself that if they could do it so could I. It was like I was a sponge, soaking up everything and then going home to put it into practice. Over time I grew stronger in myself, in confidence and self-esteem. The fog was starting to lift and I was starting to see a promising future for myself and my children.

The 12-step program was the 'official' start of my transformation. For the first time ever, things were making sense – my childhood environment, the generational impact.

Being with the group was like coming home to a family who knew exactly how I felt because they were living the same life.

Different stories but the same behaviours. Or, in my words, 'same meat, different gravy'. Once you took out the circumstances, the underlying issue was the same.

All of a sudden, I found myself having to address 'me' – my low self-esteem and my poor opinion of myself. I'd played the victim for years and now I needed to build myself up from the inside out. I had to throw out those 'masks' I'd been wearing as protection and get honest with myself. I had to stop expecting others to understand what I'd seen and experienced. My strength had to come from within.

This was where I decided to stop fighting back. It didn't mean I'd given up. Quite the opposite. I'd just decided I needed to do things in a quiet way, without the screaming and yelling.

It's a story you hear so often. After a violent outburst, he was always remorseful and things would be better for a period of time. I believed him every time he said he'd change but there were so many things that set him off.

If the meal wasn't what he wanted, it would end up on the ceiling and he'd smash plates. At first, I'd clean everything away so when he'd sobered up it was like nothing had ever happened. Later, I taught my children to walk around the broken things on the floor instead, so when he was sober he could see for himself what he'd done and I didn't need to go on a rant with all the gory details.

"Clean it up, please," I'd say, calmly and softly.

He started to see what he was like and eventually attended some AA meetings, but that didn't last long once he realised that I understood the 12-step program and could speak easily to the other members. He didn't like that and accused me of having an affair with every one of them.

Going to these meetings, something inside me changed as well. I'd started seeing him as a person to pity. It was like a light had been switched on.

It put him off guard. I wasn't giving him the reaction he needed, and he struggled with that.

I wasn't his doormat anymore.

It didn't stop him cold, but that was okay because there was something new deep inside me. A strength. An inner knowing.

I felt supported.

Through the 12-Step Program I started to grow because I was in an environment that heard me, listened to me and didn't judge me. The change didn't happen overnight; I was still living in fear of my partner finding out and accusing me of seeing someone else. I wouldn't stick around after the meeting for this reason, even though I knew he was at work and wouldn't be home for hours. His control over me was absolute.

In my mind, I did not have the knowledge to fully change things. It wasn't that simple. For years, people had been telling me to leave him – "Just walk out," they'd say. I always found excuses why I couldn't. Why I shouldn't.

Now, however, things were different. I was different, and I had support. With this support I learned to understand, rather than condemn, the alcoholic and the battle he and others in his situation go through.

Doing this, letting go of the need to condemn, allowed me to focus on myself and work to break the cycle I'd been born into. I knew it wasn't going to be easy to change the habitual behaviours from my childhood. They were like a well-worn pair of shoes – so comfortable. But I was ready. I was determined to move forward despite knowing it would be difficult at times.

Before me were two choices. I could take the easy road or I could pick myself up, dust myself off and keep going every time I was knocked down.

I chose the latter.

I was determined to break the cycle and I wanted more for my children. I'd wasted so much time, but now I was choosing to live in a more expansive mindset and achieve my potential.

This was the turning point for the rest of my life. I didn't know what it was going to look like. I did know I was going to put one foot in front of the other, wherever that was going to take me. I just had to trust that I would succeed.

As I changed, my partner was unsettled because I wasn't behaving the way he was used to. He didn't have the power over me like he once did. I could see he was struggling to be attracted to me and that eventually gave me the strength to ask him to leave my home for the second time.

He became involved with the office secretary. She'd call me up and tell me I was a horrible person to not allow him to see his children and that I should give him his share of his property. If I was her, I'd have believed everything he said too. She only wanted to see what he told her because she loved him. This is the cycle of alcoholism.

Sadly, she copped things a lot worse than I did.

I'm grateful I got out when I did.

Reflection 8

Mary Morrisey tells a story about baby elephants in India. To train them, they put a strong rope around the baby elephant's leg and attach it to a big stake in the ground. The baby elephant pulls and tugs in an effort to free itself; however, the elephant eventually gives in. It succumbs to its situation.

I was the baby elephant. I, too, gave in. I resigned myself to my situation. I followed the generational pull and continued to do what my mother did.

I am so grateful that I did attend the 12-step program because, over time, I learned I didn't have to pull and tug any more. There was an easier way forward but it wasn't outside of me – it came from within.

I was the one who had to change, not everyone around me.

I didn't need to scream and yell, hoping I'd be heard.

I had a new way of doing things, and with it the power to change my outcomes.

Interestingly, people around me were concerned I'd joined a cult. They started questioning me every time I moved. "Are you going out?" they'd say. "Where are you going?"

Rather than getting upset or frustrated, I learned that I didn't have to explain myself every time I did something different or something others were uncomfortable with.

Life became about me.

Trying new things was scary but also exciting.

I had choices.

You deserve to respect yourself.
What is a little step you could take to ensure you have control over your own life? You can start small – what is one thing you could do differently this week? What about next week? And the week after? You don't need to change the world – it is enough to join a new group, study something new or simply park somewhere different when you go to the shopping centre. The important thing is that it's your choice.

Every day the clock resets. Your wins don't matter. Your failures don't matter. Don't stress on what was, fight for what could be.
~ Sean Higgins ~

CHAPTER NINE:
Navigating ADHD

Living with my middle son was like living with two different children. He was the child I was carrying when my husband had his accident. He'd never known his father; never had that bonding experience. He'd always been that little bit trickier.

I was aware that you shouldn't compare your children, but he was so different from my other two and there were times I thought I was going crazy. As the only adult in the house, I didn't have anyone else to talk to and bounce ideas off. I was on my own.

As a baby, he wouldn't settle. So many nights were spent trying to get him to sleep.

As a toddler, it took him a long time to speak. He'd grunt when he wanted something, and when I didn't understand he'd become agitated. His sister started speaking for him.

When he got older, it was clear he had no fear. He reminded me of his father who used to get kicked out of church for sticking someone with a needle, do reckless things on his motorbike and jump off two-storey buildings.

I'll never forget the first time my son jumped off the first-level balcony of our house. My neighbour used to call out to me that he was walking along the top of the fence like a trapeze artist, and the pool fence never stopped him from getting where he wanted to be. He could clamber up and over anything, just like a monkey. To this day, I'm amazed he didn't break any bones.

He was different, I knew that much, but I couldn't put a name to it.

Year 1 was when most of the trouble started. It seemed like the phone would ring on a daily basis. "There's been an incident," the secretary, teacher or Principal would say. "Can you come down, please?"

I didn't know what to do. As a mother, I wanted to help my son. I wanted to protect him and stand by him but I had no idea what I was dealing with. All I knew was when he lost control it was to the point where it was frightening.

He didn't have an 'off switch'.

I recall being called up to the school when he was in Year 1 because he'd pulled a boy out of his way and hurt him.

"I wanted to get my schoolbag," he said when we asked why. "He was in my way and I couldn't get it." In his mind it was simple: he wanted his bag. He didn't have a way to process his actions, he just reacted.

Another time, he became so angry with a boy down the road that he picked up a brick. He was going to bash him. There was no logic. No thinking things through. Something inside him would snap and that was it. He was just a little boy; he had no idea what was going on.

The school sent us to the guidance officer who did a personality test on both of us. "You clash because you have opposite personalities," he said. That may have been true, but it certainly wasn't a useful answer for a mother trying to help her son. Nobody seemed to understand what was happening. Expert after expert ran us through different 'processes' but nobody gave me a solution.

Other families who were also struggling would enrol their children somewhere else, hoping a new school would have the solution. I was determined to find an answer to my son's situation myself, though, rather than expecting the school to fix everything. My son was a child and I was the parent – I believed it was up to me to find the answers.

It got to a point where my son became an easy target for the bullies in the school system. He would react to someone else's behaviour, but it was usually my son who was suspended or got sent to time-out. The students were very good at provoking him. When he snapped, the school would only see the end result.

Then he started running away from school. It seemed to him to be easier than dealing with his teachers not seeing the whole story.

Nobody had the time or energy to ask the right questions. I knew that running away wasn't the right thing for my son to do, but at the same time, I could understand it. I'd been there with my parents and my alcoholic partner. Some things are just in the 'too hard' basket. The victim is often the one blamed. I can understand how he must have felt, being seen as the person at fault for everything that happened.

Every day I waited and wondered, 'What next? Who will he hurt or what will he do today?' Every time my son found himself in a situation, I was called up to the school. It was extremely stressful and I knew I had to come up with a plan.

I really was flying blind trying to figure this all out on my own but it was important for me to do this. The main problem was that my son was aggressive. He would just snap. In the blink of an eye, the nearest bystander would be the recipient of his anger. It didn't matter who it was – teacher, student or family.

It took a frightening incident at home for me to finally seek outside help.

My son would lose it over what most people considered to be the smallest things, but to him they weren't small. One of these days, he had escalated to the point where he was out of control – again. It was over something minor to me but major to him. Suddenly, I found myself pressing him up against the wall with my hands around his throat. I have no idea what happened. I was horrified. I rang the GP clinic immediately and got straight in.

"If you don't find something wrong with my son," I said to my doctor, "then he's going to kill me or I'm going to kill him."

I was completely numb. Thoughts ran through my mind. What if I'd hurt him? Was I a bad mum? He's just a boy. I was supposed to be the adult.

It scared the life out of me.

His behaviour was becoming more and more volatile and I had no idea how to deal with it – that much was obvious. It was not normal behaviour.

"We can go through all the things you've already done," the doctor said, "or we can go straight to the top."

I was so relieved she believed me. "Let's go to the top," I said.

The doctor had actually listened to me. I'd tried to talk to people so many times and nobody had believed me. They'd palmed me off with 'the answer' from some textbook or theory study when they really didn't understand the problem. It wasn't helpful. I'd taken a risk by going to the doctor that day, but I'd had no choice because I knew in my heart that someone was going to get hurt.

I am so grateful my doctor heard me.

She gave me a referral to the top psychiatrist in Brisbane. "Make an appointment as soon as you can," she said.

I made the appointment and explained the reason to my son. He was okay with it. Perhaps, deep down, he knew he needed help too.

We took the train into the city, both of us rather quiet on the journey. I was wondering how it was all going to unfold. What would we find out? Was there something seriously wrong? How would I cope? My son was lost in his own thoughts. Neither of us knew what we were about to walk into.

Once we arrived, I managed to find our way out of the station and to the building that housed the psychiatrist's office. My son said nothing this whole time. As we stepped out of the lift, he looked up at me.

"It'll be okay," I said. I hoped I was right. We needed answers.

The office was empty when we walked in. It wasn't elaborate or fancy but it was nice. Cosy and welcoming. We sat and waited in silence. I knew enough not ask my son random questions or try to engage him in conversation when he was like this. Doing that would set him off.

A door opened and a man stepped out with another person. He nodded in my direction. "I'll be with you shortly," he said.

It felt good to be acknowledged.

After he'd made an appointment for the other person and they'd left, the psychiatrist turned to me again and introduced himself. "Please come in," he said, opening the door for us.

I walked through and, thankfully, my son followed me.

"Now," the psychiatrist said once we'd all sat down, "tell me what's been going on."

He had a friendly face. Serious but open. I felt like I could trust him. While my son sat, quiet and with his head down, I explained what had been happening. The behaviours. My fears. Everything.

The psychiatrist listened.

Then he explained what we were going to do moving forward. Tests. Assessments. Diagnosis.

The first thing he had us do, right then, was answer a questionnaire. The psychiatrist stayed in the office with my son and I was sent outside to the waiting area to fill in my sheet.

It was 'tick and flick'; multiple choice. There were questions about personality, sleeping habits and reactions to a range of situations.

Then the psychiatrist said he'd be sending my son for a range of tests. "They're designed to help us get clarity about what is going on," he explained. "They'll also eliminate other things."

One of these tests was an electroencephalogram (EEG). They put a weird-looking cap on my son's head and connected wires to it. "It's to check his brainwave activity," they said.

I was so proud of my son. He did everything he was asked to do. While we were talking, he sat quietly and played with his bum bag.

This bag was like his security blanket. He wore it everywhere he went and didn't allow anyone to touch it. Even if we were going out somewhere that required my son to be dressed nicely, he still had to have this bum bag with him. He'd tuck it under his shirt.

The bag was filled with items he'd collected – stones, sticks and even the tabs from shopping bags at the checkout. I never saw him pick these items up, but his bag was full of them.

"Obsessive-compulsive disorder," the psychiatrist said. "OCD."

The tests went on and on, but that was fine. I saw it all as a process we both had to go through to get the answers needed to help my son.

Once the tests were all done we had to wait weeks for all the results to be collated so a diagnosis could be made. It felt like forever. Then, finally, I got a call from our GP. "The results are back," she said. "Let's get you in to talk about them."

On the drive over to the doctor's my son was very quiet. We both were. Again we sat in the waiting room in silence. When our names were called, we walked in – both of us a bit hesitant. I had no inkling of what the outcome would be and what it would mean for my son. For both of us.

"Take a seat." Our doctor smiled, warm and welcoming as always. She had a thick wad of papers in front of her, which she shuffled through as she talked. She went through each of the tests and explained the different results.

Then came the one result we'd been waiting for.

"He has severe attention deficit hyperactivity disorder," she said.

ADHD. I'd heard of it but didn't know much about it.

She explained about the different levels. "He's below the lowest line," she said, pointing to the graph. "Here."

I had no idea what it all meant. I was just relieved we finally had a name for what was going on.

It wasn't until later, after we got home, that it hit me.

What now?

At our next appointment with the psychiatrist, he gave me a stack of information to take home and read through. There was a lot to take in, but I wanted to know more so I did lots of my own research as well. I'd been told we had a choice of two medications – Ritalin or dexamphetamine. Both were restricted medications and both had side effects that were rather scary. I wanted to make an informed decision.

Restricted medications have to be authorised by the government in Canberra, and patients are closely monitored to make sure they are only taking what is prescribed. Not knowing anything different, I trusted the professionals and accepted the direction of the psychiatrist. He put my son on dexamphetamine tablets, the one with the lesser side effects. I was given all the known information about this medication, including the strict rules and regulations about its usage.

I recognised that the dexamphetamine calmed my son down, but there was so much more to it. You can't give a child a tablet and think everything will be alright and I didn't feel comfortable just leaving it at this. I needed to find out as much as I could about ADHD. There had to be more to all of this. I asked lots of questions. What causes ADHD? Was it hereditary? Was it caused by the stress I was under when I was pregnant?

Then, I had an epiphany.

Even if I knew the cause, was this going to change what I was dealing with right here and right now? The answer was a resounding "NO!" The most important thing was finding out how I could help my son succeed – without being solely reliant on restricted medications.

After further research and discussions with my son's doctors, I came to understand that the role of the medication was to calm my son's aggression so he could focus. Knowing this gave me the opportunity to explore strategies and techniques that worked for him. It was a trial-and-error process as so little was known about ADHD in the 80s, let alone alternative treatments for it.

I approached the school to see if they'd be willing for us to work together to help my son.

They were.

I'd been attending a group called 'Tough Love'. The main thing this group taught us was that we needed to support each other. It taught us to listen and gave us permission to be heard. Essentially, one parent would share their story – we could vent and get it all out – while the others would just listen. Then, the parent who'd spoken would be given a zipper. This meant they needed to sit quietly while the other parents suggested strategies to try for one week. From the suggestions, the parent could then select one or two strategies they were willing to trial for the following week.

I asked the school if they'd be willing to try something similar.

Every time my son got himself in a situation we'd bring in everyone involved in the incident, including teachers and students – basically, anyone who was affected by what my son did. We'd have a meeting where we'd all come together – students, parent, teacher, Deputy Principal. Everyone had the opportunity to speak without being interrupted. The school would say what their concerns were and what they needed. Then it was our turn – me and my son.

Over time, this worked well. Eventually, this process helped my son see the bigger picture and understand how his choices contributed to the situation and related to his ultimate punishment. He was able to understand the core issue and could see who his actions affected and how. It didn't end when he came home; I had him write about what happened in as much detail as possible. He began to see and, more importantly, articulate the impact he had on others through the choices he made. He could also come up with a better scenario, one that would give him the best results. Of course, he still had to deal with the consequences of his behaviour at school but now he understood why.

The school started using other strategies. We came up with a card system – a red card which gave my son the opportunity to be in control of his own outcome. It wasn't a 'get out of class free' card, and he knew he was only to use it if he found himself getting agitated. He'd let the teacher know and was allowed to go to the office and sit in a specific chair.

Everyone knew not to talk to him when he was using his red card – not even to say hello – because doing so would send him even further down the rabbit hole to a place where he had no control over his actions. The best thing was to give him space and time, allowing the chemical reaction in his body to subside.

I also supported time-out at lunch time. It was up to me when that time-out period finished because I was required to sign a letter to approve his release. Ultimately though, this was up to my son in terms of how much responsibility he was prepared to accept and how well we'd worked together to sort through what had happened. With my help, he started to recognise his energy and determine what he needed to do to pull himself up before he crossed that line of no return.

The consistency and repetition of what we were doing, along with the stable messaging and processes, were having a positive impact on my son.

As a mother, it's all you can hope for.

I am grateful to the primary school for working with me and being open to doing things in a different way. However, the constant phone calls and battles took their toll and patience was frequently in short supply.

There were, of course, difficulties and obstacles beyond what was happening at school. My other children saw it as him getting away with things they wouldn't have been able to get away with. They complained that I spent too much time dealing with my son's issues and not enough with them. I understood this. It was a natural reaction.

Other parents often didn't 'get it'. I recall going camping with friends. We'd been away with this family many times before, but this time the father said, "He's just a normal boy."

Normal? What is that?

For me, 'normal' was the raging, angry boy who scared the life out of me because I never knew what he was likely to do.

Unfortunately, this dad got to experience 'normal' firsthand on this trip. My son went into a rage over an incident. That dad never questioned my thinking ever again.

There were definitely times I was ready to give up. I was trying to finish my own education, care for my kids, keep house and help my son. It was hard work, but my determination to succeed was stronger than my desire to take the easy road.

I was just being a mum trying to help her son.

I'm so glad I persevered.

Reflection 9

It surprises me today how I already knew that the answers to my son's problem came from inside him. I just didn't have a name for it back then. When he tapped into the power within himself, he started to recognise how much more control he had when it came to his outcomes.

Everything stemmed from him being consciously aware of what was happening inside himself. If he wanted different outcomes, then he needed to take control of his life by putting techniques and strategies in place that would support him to succeed.

Our thoughts and feelings are the things that help us awaken the answers and learn so much about ourselves.

When reflecting with the psychiatrist about the progress my son had made, he was amazed how my son managed to take control of his life using the tools and techniques I taught him. We all have this power if we decide to tap into it.

The insight and awareness I've received through questioning myself and my beliefs, along with the alternate modalities I use, astound me every day. I thought I knew where things came from and why I did certain things.

I was wrong.

Stepping into these deep, dark imprints gave me clarity and understanding about people and where the wounds of our childhood come from.

Our subconscious imprints are so powerful. They impact our lives and the lives of our loved ones so readily.

How often do you reflect on your standards and values? What life skills are you teaching your children? What are you silently telling your children or, if you're a teacher, the students you work with?

Are you ready to take the necessary steps to have better outcomes?

_____

The only limitations are ones we put on ourselves.
~ Ita Buttrose ~

_____

CHAPTER TEN:
Back to School as a Mature Age Student

Having taken that step to leave my partner, I was now raising three small children on my own. The difference this time was that I had support from my 12-step family.

Nobody told me what to do. Nobody condemned me or judged my decisions – not even when I took him back for a time. They accepted me and my choices, and that is what made it easier.

Once I ended the relationship, he didn't have that control over me anymore. I wasn't frightened of him. I had come to know myself and realised I deserved better.

Still, for a long time he could reel me into a phone conversation. He would ring me and tell me he loved me. He could be really nice and then suddenly gut me like a fish, leaving me devastated all over again.

Over time, I was sucked into his games less and less. I began recognising the point where the conversation started to turn and would come up with some sort of excuse about needing to go. "I have to go to the toilet", "The children are calling" or "Someone is at the door," I said whatever it took to get off that call and avoid giving him the reaction he desired.

The biggest question on my mind was 'How am I going to move forward?'

I didn't want to be on government support for the rest of my life. I wanted more for my children; more for me. I was determined to be a good role model for my children, showing them that it is possible to do and be whatever you want; that you can achieve anything when you know how.

I'd grown up with the stigma of living in a housing commission house. I knew what other people thought of those of us who received government assistance.

I didn't want that anymore – especially for my children.

My parents never owned their own home, but I did. It was a positive first step and I knew how fortunate I was. Next, I had to work out how I was going earn money with no education or skills to speak of and three children to support.

Then I saw it. An article in the local newspaper: 'Mature age students head back to high school'. I read it from beginning to end. Then I read it again.

Could I do this?

I certainly had the desire to change and to make the most of new opportunities. So, I swallowed back my fear and my memories of failure and rang the school.

The Principal was very understanding. And welcoming. He asked me to take a seat and explained how everything works for mature age students. I explained I wanted to return to school to complete my high school education.

"Try it for six months," he suggested, "and see if it's for you."

I took a deep breath. "Yes," I said. "I'll do it."

That was the easy part.

Stepping back into education after being out of school for over a decade was an eye-opener. Teaching styles and even the content had changed so much. I was learning things I'd never heard of when I was at school in the 60s.

I wasn't the oldest mature age student; ages ranged from mid-twenties to fifty-plus years. Thankfully, we didn't have to wear the school uniform. We were also allocated our own study room so we didn't have to sit in the playground with the teenagers.

The whole experience was exhilarating. It was also scary as all my insecurities came back, bubbling away below the surface.

We attended classes with the regular high school kids. The first few times I rocked up to a classroom and stood waiting in line with twenty to thirty teenage students was a bit odd. Some of the younger students embraced the opportunity. Others were not thrilled. Some students refused to work with the 'oldies' and others loved it.

Oddly enough, some of the students who refused to speak to me or work with me in a group would be totally friendly when they saw me outside of school. The complexity of human nature never failed to intrigue me.

It wasn't easy but having the time with other mature age students during the lunch break really helped.

One of my biggest hurdles was my first exam. All those childhood fears came rushing back to me.

You can't do this.

You'll fail.

Get up and run out that door; never look back.

That voice – the very one that had controlled me most of my life – was incessant. It wasn't giving up and it was reluctant to release its hold on me.

But I had a new voice – a voice that believed in me.

I had people who believed me and told me I could do this.

I would see this through.

I'm so pleased I stayed planted on the seat, even with my heart racing and the constant negative voice in my head. I'm so pleased I made a choice for me. A choice that would see me through to succeed.

I breathed deeply and focused on the exam questions, blocking out my inner fight, and I completed that exam. I had no idea whether I'd passed or not, but at that moment it wasn't that important. I'd won, no matter the outcome, because I'd stayed and seen it through.

That was the first time I stepped beyond my fear and challenged those old habitual thoughts that had held me back for such a long time. I'd made the first step of many towards my future life. 'If I could do this,' I wondered, 'what else am I capable of doing?'

My history would not define who I was now.

There was a fine line to tread between being an adult and being a student. Determining 'right' from 'wrong' wasn't as easy as it may seem. One time, we were waiting for the teacher to arrive. It got later and later and still no teacher. The 'right' thing to do would have been to go to the front office and inform them we had no teacher. As the new kid on the block, however, I realised it was best to go with the flow if I knew what was good for me. I may have been an adult, but these students were still my peers and acceptance was important. I stood with all the others and waited.

Juggling homework and assignments with housework and caring for my children wasn't easy but I was determined to see it through. Most of the time my kids were fine with me being at school, although my daughter did not want me at the same school as her. "You better be finished before I get there," she said, more than once. "It would be so embarrassing if you weren't."

My middle son was also being problematic. It was nothing to do with me being at school but that extra load added to the stress. He was having his own issues at school and I was having to juggle his behaviours in the mix with everything else.

Still, I pushed on – for me and for my kids. I needed to show them, especially my middle son, that nothing could stand in their way if they were determined to achieve a goal.

In terms of the work, there was content I'd never seen before. The standard was way more advanced than I remembered. Reading was something I struggled with. Maths, in particular, was incredibly difficult. I couldn't seem to retain new information. The teachers' instructions and explanations would often go in one ear and out the other.

Eventually, I decided I needed a maths tutor if I was to have any hope of succeeding. It was one of the best decisions I've made. My tutor was so helpful and understanding. The way he explained things made sense. More than anything else, he gave me new confidence and a mindset that I could do this.

I recall the first exam I had to sit. All those childhood fears came rushing to the surface – you'll fail, you can't do this, you'll be laughed at when you fail, better get up and leave. All of these thoughts kept running through my head. If I didn't have a different way of thinking, it's quite possible I'd have up and run, like another mature age student did.

Instead, I stayed. I completed that exam. I kept going.

I was amazed to discover I'd managed to score half a mark off 'full marks' on a test.

"Go on," one of the kids said to the teacher, "let her have full marks." The other students echoed the request.

The teacher stood by his marking. I respected that, but I was honoured that the students fought for me. It was something I'd never experienced before.

Each time I stepped beyond my comfort level, I grew in confidence.

My English teacher set an assignment to do a book review. The fear rose in me, that little voice telling me I couldn't do the assignment, that I'd fail because my reading wasn't good. Previously I would have sat there and let the fear consume me. I would never have had the courage to approach a teacher to ask for help for fear of being ridiculed.

But that was then.

After class I approached my teacher. "I can't do this," I said.

"Yes, you can," he replied. "I'll help you."

He set me a task each night to read for five to ten minutes. I was then to come to his staffroom the next day at lunch time and explain what I'd read. Breaking the task down into manageable chunks helped me get through. I'd never had anyone sit down and take the time to do something like that for me.

I completed that book review.

Another fear I had was public speaking. The idea of having to stand up in front of my class and speak on a certain topic terrified me. Luckily, the scope of the topic was very broad so I selected something close to my heart – living with domestic violence.

My teacher was amazed. "For someone so quiet," she said, "your speech was amazing."

Who would have thought I could do all of these things? But I did.

I graduated high school at the age of thirty-three.

At graduation I received the Commerce Award and a wonderful reference:

> *Tracey is a highly respected adult student whose dedication*
> *and commitment to her personal goals is exceptional.*
> *Tracey has managed to confidently deal with the demands*
> *of study alongside her family commitments.*

Trying to get an education as a mature age student is not easy at the best of times. When you're the sole parent to three school-aged children, it's harder. It's a real balancing act.

At times I wanted to throw in the towel because it was so hard navigating everything on my own.

I'm so glad I didn't.

Reflection 10

I am always astonished how our childhood imprints impact our thoughts as we go through life.

I believed I did not have the ability to do anything other than be a clothes sorter. I believed I wasn't deserving of anything more. How wrong I was.

For me, this thinking was generational. It was part of a cycle of thought I'd been born into.

I was determined to break this cycle for my children. Of course, they'd also been affected by already living in the same environment as I had for the majority of their childhood.

Blame is something you can't afford to entertain. I used to blame myself but have learned not to anymore. If you don't know anything different, you can't change things.

The learning curve was huge. Was I doing the right thing or the wrong thing? All I could do was try. If I failed, I had to try again. Having a sponsor to support me in the 12-step program was wonderful because I no longer felt alone. I had someone to reason things out with, someone who listened and someone who allowed me to make my own decisions.

My aim was to help my children see a different way, even though – like I was before them – they were so comfortable with the status quo.

> *Think about your status quo.*
> *Are you comfortable with the way things are or are you ready to do things differently and move forward to improved outcomes? Making that decision is the first step. You deserve more and can have more.*
> *You have the power to change your outcomes if you are ready and willing to step beyond what you know.*

You have the power.
~ Mary Morrissey ~

CHAPTER ELEVEN:
My Change and My Kids

The whole point of my transformation was to benefit my children; to break the cycle so they didn't have to experience my life. However, the change was difficult for my children who had been conditioned from birth to survive in a very dysfunctional environment.

As I explored who I wanted to be, my children fought me every step of the way and we locked horns on a daily basis.

Housework, shopping, gardening, cleaning the pool, mowing the grass – I was only one person and had to depend on my children to a point when it came to maintaining the house. They were kids. They wanted to be kids. It was hard for them to understand how much I was struggling, trying to manage volatile situations with my son's ADHD and focusing on getting an education myself.

It wasn't just the chores, though – the tension went deeper than that.

It was the alcoholic-dominated life they'd been experiencing since birth.

Alcoholism creates a very controlling and manipulative environment. Everyone involved behaves both like a parent and a child. One minute they want to control others, the next minute they're throwing tantrums. My children learned this behaviour through watching me and my interactions with my partner in the same way that I learned by watching my parents.

I created the situation because I couldn't do absolutely everything. When the children didn't get their way or wanted to take back the control they'd move into 'poor me' or the blame game. It was always someone else's fault.

And so we battled.

I believed it was my role to help my children learn to use all appliances. When they went out in the world I wanted them to be self-sufficient – not like my neighbour's husband who didn't know how to use the washing machine. When my neighbour passed away he was lost; she'd always done everything around the house. I didn't want my children to be like this.

I understand how hard it must have been for them. Children need to be children. My children didn't have that opportunity.

What came out of that situation was my eldest regularly stepping into the role of parent. I can still see her laying down the law to her brothers.

Problems arose when I wanted to be the parent, though. My daughter probably felt I didn't need her anymore, or that she wasn't good enough. It reminded me of how I felt when my mother re-mopped the floor I'd just cleaned.

My children resisted because they believed I was trying to change them. I was trying to reinvent their lives. Everything about my new behaviour was utterly foreign. They were comfortable with how things had been; they knew how to react to those situations. Suddenly, I was turning everything upside down and inside out on them.

Change is challenging for everyone concerned, especially when people don't understand or feel the need for change. It was me who was struggling with where I came from. My children had so much more than I did as a child. That's not their fault. All parents want to give their children more. In my case, however, my 'more' had become the life skills to create something beyond what I'd been born into. There was no choice for my children, and that's the hard bit – they just had to come along for the ride.

What a ride it was!

And not a good one.

As a parent you set boundaries, but every boundary I set she would push back. If we were going out, she'd step in. "Hurry up, you two," she'd say to her brothers. She'd become used to doing this when I was busy studying and found it hard not to continue taking over.

Then she found it hard when I tried telling her what to do.

I don't blame anyone.

What I'm doing is recognising how we can all get caught up in 'the cycle' because we don't know anything different.

With three children, there was always an imbalance. It's often this way in families – two against one. In our case, the major denominator was my daughter; she always wanted to be the 'mother' and, if I'm completely honest, I did put her in that position at times. When I did try to be mother, she fought, she resisted and she brought her brothers along with her. She was always in and one of the boys would be out. This was the control she had. For me, taking back that control as the parent was so hard. Sadly this is what eventually tore our family apart. I could see what was happening, but no matter how hard I tried to bring us all together it just didn't work. Outside forces.

Nothing came easily. Single mum. Three young children, one with severe ADHD. Attending school. Maintaining a home. There were many times I wanted to give up, but I also wanted to change my future and knew I wouldn't happen if I didn't continue to put one foot in front of the other. I needed to keep moving forward. I didn't know where forward was or what it led to, but I did know that no matter what, I wasn't going to go backwards. As long as I kept taking steps it didn't matter how small or slow they were.

One particular time I came extremely close to walking out on my study goals. My son had been out of control at school, misbehaving and running away. The phone would ring on an almost daily basis. Then one day, after yet another phone call, I was so overwhelmed by constantly having to do everything on my own that I went to one of my teachers.

"I think it would be best if I give up and stay home," I said. "I need to look after my children."

The teacher just looked at me for a moment. "And what about you?" she said.

What about me, indeed? They were the exact words I needed to hear.

After this short conversation I realised that for me to survive the challenge of home and study I needed a structured routine where we all had chores to do. I knew the structure would be good for my children, too. Plus, they'd learn some life skills along the way.

Not everyone agreed with my choices or what I was doing. I told myself that 'old Tracey' would have been terribly wounded by the opinions and behaviours of others, but 'new Tracey' wasn't about to allow that to happen.

'Old Tracey' let fear rule her life. She'd get in a car with him when he'd been drinking because she was afraid. Not for her life. She was afraid of being left to raise her children alone. She was afraid of not having enough food to feed her family. Irrational fears stopped her in her tracks every time.

'New Tracey' refused to listen to her fears. That alone was terrifying in itself, but I knew I had choices. My fear would no longer keep me limited or rise up to consume me. Some tried to 'punish' me by ignoring me or not inviting me to things, but I refused to let that get me down for long. I was entitled to my choices. They were mine.

As I grew into my new skin, I began to stand up and be heard. Some people were not comfortable with this new me. I even had my ex-partner's parents accuse me of being in a cult – all because I'd started to respect myself. Some people started to ignore me and eventually reject me because they couldn't cope. All that did was tell me I was moving forward and breaking free from those shackles I was born into.

Then there was the name-calling when I was a teenager. Stress meant I couldn't gain weight, and I'd hear people say that going to bed with me would be like going to bed with a bag of bones.

Moving forward also meant coming across people in business and networking situations who were threatened by the new me. I didn't fit into their 'mould'. I'd find myself not being acknowledged when I went into a room. I joined a group and paid my money, yet wasn't acknowledged at all for over six months. It doesn't bother me anymore because I've realised that the people that I do attract are the people I want to work with and support in their endeavours.

I used to have to wear a different face for different situations. Not anymore. I'm proud of who I am and who I'm becoming.

There is still so much more to learn about myself, and I'm open to the challenge.

I don't have to put others down to make myself look good.

I don't feel the need to fight back if others undermine me.

I'm not a sheep anymore. I have a voice, but I know when to step away for my own mental health and wellbeing.

What I have learned is I need to stay true to my standards and behaviours, and if others don't have the courage to stand up for what is right that is their issue.

Principles over personalities! I follow this practice and have tried to instil it into my children – we look at what is right rather than who is right.

I understand what my values and principles are. I don't change direction depending on who I'm with. I try to be consciously aware of what comes out of my mouth.

We live in a world of blame. I am over blaming other people for what happens to me in my life. The only person I can blame if things are not working out for me is ME.

I have the power to walk away. I've always had the power to choose, I just didn't realise it was there. I can choose who I want in my life and who I don't. I don't need to wait around to be accepted by nasty, manipulative people.

Reflection 11

What I learned as a child impacted my own children. Whether good or bad, children learn from what they see.

One of the things I had to do was forgive myself, which was not easy because I was so busy forgiving and allowing everything that others would do and say. It was definitely uncomfortable when I had to put myself first.

What might've happened if I'd given up my education again and stayed home with my children? Would I be living a different life? Would they? I suspect we'd all be on the same old merry-go-round.

Even now, I see us jumping on that ride every so often. For many years there was a huge rift between my sisters, just like there was a huge rift between my mother and her family and, years later, that same rift between me and my children. It was like watching a movie on continual repeat. The reasons for the rift were all similar, too – they were about control and manipulation.

They were also about rejection. Or the perception of rejection.

No-one wants to be rejected, but often what we think of as rejection is actually a choice made by someone else who has the right to choose what they want in their life.

Feeling rejected rather than accepting another's choice is a learned behaviour. Judgement is a learned response. Blame is a learned response. I learned how to react from my parents, as they learned from theirs and my children learned for me. The difference is there's no blame now from me. Instead, there's an acknowledgement of a lack of awareness.

That acknowledgement is empowering.

And it allows me to invest in myself and take control of my life.

Every step you take can bring you closer to your dream.
I know this because I decided I was deserving and worth more, even when I didn't know what 'more' was at the time I started my journey.
What about you? Are you living the same life over and over again because it's the easier path? Or do you want to start reaching for your dreams?

Our greatest weakness lies in giving up. The most certain way to succeed is always to try just one more time.
- Thomas A Edison -

CHAPTER TWELVE:
Finding My Wings to Success

Towards the end of Year 12 we were all asked to think about where we saw ourselves in five or ten years.

I couldn't answer because I didn't know. Even when I thought about it, I had no idea. I'd been focused on just getting through each day, one step at a time; I hadn't even considered the future.

Getting my education had been my goal, but I'd done so without a vision of where it would take me. I hadn't realised how essential that vision was or that, even if it wasn't clear, we all needed to have one. I was moving, but not heading anywhere.

For most of my life I hadn't even known who I was as an individual. When I'd entered the 12-Step Program, it was the first time I'd ever thought about who I was.

Who was Tracey?

What did Tracey want? What did Tracey like? What did she want to become?

I had no idea.

As I came closer to completing my education the second time around, one of the teachers said, "What do you want to do now?"

I didn't know!

Up until that point, I'd just existed. It didn't matter what I liked or who I wanted to become, I was just there and had to be content with what was in front of me. Other people's needs and wants had to be considered before my own.

I rolled my car once. My children were in it. I'd spent the day supporting my parents as they dealt with reading my grandparents' wills. Not only had I driven them there and back, but I also felt compelled to please my sister by going out on a boat for half a day with her and two guys. I was exhausted. There was every chance I could have paid the ultimate price just because of my need to please everyone else. Nobody was hurt, but that doesn't take away what might have been. The thought that I could have killed all of us by not looking after myself was something I've never forgotten.

Now I'd found myself with the opportunity to focus on who I was as a person. It was time to treasure my life first and foremost – because if I didn't, who would?

After some thought, I realised I'd extended myself so much in those three years leading up to graduation. It had been tiring. Dealing with my son's ADHD while studying and raising three children was a lot to take on. I decided to take a gap year before stepping into my university studies.

The school I graduated from offered me a job working in the office. I loved it, and it also served as a stark reminder of what I could've had if I'd remained at school the first time round. Who knows? With a different environment I may have been a personal assistant, but I hadn't given myself the opportunity to find out because I'd caved in to the pull of my past.

One day very early on in my gap year, the Principal said, "Most people don't return after taking a break."

I could've listened to those words and allowed them to define my outcomes. But no. I was ready and willing to continue to go forth and find my true purpose and passion.

During my journey of self-discovery I learned to step back and be conscious of 'me' – my behaviours, my thoughts and my feelings. My intuition started to grow and tapped into my internal voice. It forced me to truly listen to what I wanted for myself.

This internal voice was the voice of my true essence, calling me to follow my heart and my dreams. It wanted me to recognise my potential, because throughout my life I'd always let others decide what I did, said and became. Not anymore. It was time for things to be about me, rather than others. It was time to put my needs first and everyone else's next.

My thoughts would no longer hold me back. They would stop telling me I wasn't deserving.

The first big goal I set myself was to go to a café after the 12-Step meeting so I could have a hot chocolate. I was shaking in my boots, terrified my partner would find out and that I'd be in real trouble.

If anybody knew about this fear, they'd think I was nuts. It was just a hot chocolate! For me, though, walking through the café door and ordering that hot chocolate was like climbing the biggest, steepest mountain and not knowing if I would make it to the top and back down again alive.

I was fearful that fear would take over. It had many times before but I was a different person now. I was evolving into a remarkably strong lady who was driven to change her outcomes for the sake of her mental health and her children.

I got my hot chocolate.

And I enjoyed it.

That day, I truly recognised myself as an individual. Not a mum. Not a partner. Not a wife. I was Tracey. I didn't just need to get my hot chocolate – I needed to get that individual back for good.

Finally, I was ready to change my outcomes for the better.

I deserved more and I could have more.

It was time to be kind to me, not just to others.

It was 'me-time', and I was ready to shine brightly for me!

That individual – the real Tracey – was incredibly difficult to find. I'd spent a lifetime being the person people expected me to be. A lifetime living in fear people would find out what went on – all the fighting and arguments – behind my family's closed doors.

If I was in a relationship, the face I wore was faked happiness. I had to put makeup on to hide the bruises. At the shopping centre I avoided people, and I never answered the door at home or got to know my neighbours in case someone worked out what was going on.

The purpose of everything I did – hiding, pushing people away – was to keep myself safe and to keep everyone happy. Not necessarily in that order, though.

I put so much pressure on me.

All those fears of being 'found out' and deemed 'unworthy' stopped me from being me. They would rise up and send me scuttling back to what I knew and what was comfortable. It kept me stuck and allowed my family and others to bully and intimidate me. I wouldn't stand up for myself; instead, I backed down and did what other people told or expected me to do.

Challenging that thinking was – and is – scary. It took many, many attempts, a conscious effort and a strong inner voice to overcome it.

Often I found myself slipping into my comfort zone again, fear of the consequences putting me back on autopilot. It was a habitual response. I had to grow a thinking brain; one that allowed me to pull myself up consciously and recognise the direction I was taking. I needed to know when I was on the old path and remind myself it was a path I didn't want to go down anymore. It was up to me to do the mental exercises to keep me on the right path.

I had the power to stop everything in its tracks.

It was key for me to start recognising behaviours as habits. In the process of training myself to see these I came to see the habits in my life, such as my reactions and the results of these reactions. Often when I was scared or fearful, particularly when it came to the actions of my ex-partner, I'd find myself going on a rant – which, in itself, did nothing to solve the issue. Once I recognised this I started using a diversion tactic, like focusing on a book, to stop my reactions. After a while, this worked and my partner stopped doing things that had once instigated a reaction from me.

By changing my behaviour, the outcome also changed.

You can't control others. You can only control you.

Persistence was essential. It took time, but I got better and better at doing things differently. I stopped getting angry at myself for reacting or caving into fear. Instead, I reflected.

My behaviours and reactions were so ingrained I just 'did' them without thinking.

Now, I was questioning every little thing I did or thought. The answers I came back with kept me from going back to my old normal.

This part of my life was like being on a swing. I'd go forward. I'd go back. Great swooping arches, over and over. My hands gripped tight onto a thin chain – the thread of my life. Each time I sailed forward I faced the threat of flying off the swing, of moving too fast and heading out of control. Yet, each time I sailed back that same fear threatened to dump me, face down, in a defeated heap.

Over time, the swing's distance shortened. Moving forward and going back merged into one. The more I explored who I was, the more I stepped outside my comfort zone, the more empowered I became.

It was overwhelming at times. My heart raced a million miles an hour. A lump formed in my throat. At first, I feared these sensations. Then, over time, I came to embrace them as a sign that I was expanding my scope and challenging my abilities within new arenas.

The pull to give up and accept the easy road remains, yet the trust and belief that I can push on and move past that invisible boundary tells me I will succeed.

I'd already spent many years getting to know 'me' – who I was. What I'd never considered, though, was who I wanted to become. I'd never asked myself that before, so I now set my sites on doing just that.

I began considering everything, right down to the simplest things in my life – all the little things I cherished then and still cherish today. I became very reflective and was always mulling over those questions: who was I and who did I want to become?

In this reflective space, I would watch people to observe qualities I liked and didn't like. I questioned the negative qualities and asked myself whether I had them and, if so, what the opposite was. I wanted to become aware of all these negative traits so I could eliminate them from the person I wanted to become. I watched positive qualities in people and tried them on to see how they looked on me. It was a process, one that I continue to use today as I evolve into the person I am becoming.

Things would come to me at the most unexpected times.

One day I was doing some weeding. I love being outside, surrounded by nature, so weeding was never a chore. A wonderful willie wagtail decided to join me as I kneeled there. He flitted around and came up really close. It gave me so much pleasure to see how brave he was; it was like he instinctively knew he could trust me.

I realised that I wanted that same instinctiveness. I wanted to grow and nurture that internal knowing we all have if we decide to step into that space and believe in that voice. An intuition I was not connected to at that time but wanted in the future.

This led me to reflect on my journey and recognise that my inner voice was speaking to me all along but I didn't hear it because I wasn't listening. I thought I had all the answers but those answers only took me down the rabbit hole of repetition, disappointment and hurt.

Although I still had those moments, I was on a new journey and it was exciting. I knew I had a choice – I could either step away or I could get caught up in the old cycle.

I'd never had a man in my life who respected me because I hadn't learned to love myself as a person, warts and all. Realising this was an eye-opening moment and it led me to further realise that it didn't only apply to love and relationships but to my life in general. I wasn't going to get anywhere until I started to believe there was something amazing I was supposed to do. Something that was inside me and wanted to bust out and be seen. The true me. A person I could admire and respect.

Even though I didn't know what it was, I knew there would be something. I knew there was more for me. I just needed to continue looking forward and believing.

Getting to know me was really uncomfortable because I didn't know what love was, I didn't know how to love myself, let alone someone else.

A group I attended posed the question: what do you like about yourself? We only had to say one thing. Just one.

I couldn't do it.

I really struggled. It was like speaking a foreign language. Of course, I wimped out and copied someone else's answer. When it was my turn I said, "My hair." I didn't like it either but at least it was an answer.

Today I can think of many attributes I like about myself. I am kind. I am caring. And I do love my hair.

That's just the tip of the iceberg.

As I grow into the person I am meant to be, that list keeps on growing. All I'd ever done was give myself away and succumb to what others expected me to do and be for them. I'd never taken the opportunity to carve my own identity; I had no idea what I was capable of or who I wanted to be.

No wonder I couldn't answer that question.

It was time to give myself to me, but how was I going to do this?

One step at a time. With trust. With belief. With perseverance.

Find someone who can help you to be the best version of yourself. I don't mean someone who will tell you what you want to hear. I mean someone who will challenge you to see beyond your circumstances, to see what in truly in your heart.

Trust in that internal voice called intuition.

It is a wonderful guide. In my life today, I don't dismiss that internal feeling. Good or bad, there is a message for me if I listen.

Reflection 12

We often don't recognise that the small steps we are taking are moving us forward until we stop and look back. Only then can we see how far we've truly come. It reminds me of my guide on the Milford Track who said, "Stop and look back; it gives you a different perspective."

Looking back gives you that perspective on how much you have grown, and that gives you the strength to keep moving forward.

Doing the work I do now shows me how many people live a default life, year in and year out, with very little change. They believe they don't deserve better. I know this because I had those same thoughts: I'm not deserving; I can't; I don't have time. The list goes on.

The thing is, we're all deserving. We all have the ability to step past the fears and doubts and into that space of 'anything is possible'.

I am grateful today because I have a voice and I know how to use it. I am grateful today because when manipulative bullies cross my path I am strong enough not to get sucked into their lies and games. And I am grateful today because I have found others who are aligned with my thinking and my values. You can't change others, but you can decide which people you want in your life.

Now, as I work with my clients I help them get greater clarity of what they would love for their life – what it looks like, how it feels and how to step into it.

Most people are sceptical of this type of believing. My clients that truly step into this space experience amazing transformation of their lives, circumstances and situations. This is the reason I love doing what I do.

We all have an internal power to change our outcomes.
What are you willing to do differently to change your life?
What would you truly love for your future? Are you ready
to step away from people who drag you down? It all starts
with a thought that you create in your imagination.

*Change the way you look at things, and
the things you look at change.*
~ Wayne W Dyer ~

CHAPTER THIRTEEN:
Stepping Into a New Version of Myself

During an in-flight safety presentation, passengers are told that if the mask on the aeroplane drops down you should fit it to yourself first before helping someone else. If you don't, you won't have enough air, and therefore you won't be able help anyone else.

It took me a long time to grasp this concept because, in my world, everyone and everything came before me. The alcoholic came first. My children came first. My family came first. I was always the last to receive, right down to small things like buying myself underwear. It wasn't easy to change habits from a lifestyle I'd been living for years.

However, I made small changes and those small changes eventually turned into bigger changes as I became more confident. I started to venture out. I started to respect myself. It was now up to me to decide who and what I wanted in my life.

My children were still young, so I found a babysitter and I went to the city once a month with some girlfriends. We'd make a night of it. I'd grown so much I didn't feel guilty. I didn't feel I shouldn't or I couldn't. I didn't worry about what others would think.

The negative talk in my head never left me alone until I made the decision to do things a different way. I had a brain, and I could now think for myself.

Going out and being an individual for the first time in my life was so enlivening. I put in place a structure I was comfortable with. My children were safe at home with the babysitter, so I didn't have to worry and I could enjoy myself.

It wasn't about going out and getting drunk and writing myself off. I didn't need alcohol to have a good time. It was about the change in me giving me more confidence every time I stepped outside my comfort zone. The pull that once kept me going back to what I knew now pulled me towards trying new things and living my life. As scary and uncomfortable as it was for a long time, the more I stepped into this new me the more I changed my outcomes.

I loved to people-watch, particularly at singles events. I'd sit and watch both the men and the women. People-watching gave me ideas about the qualities I was looking for in a male, as well as qualities I saw and admired in females. With the latter, I'd make a conscious effort to replicate those qualities and actions in my everyday life.

One quality I admired in others was their ability to take pride in their appearance and to dress nicely in a way that made them appear confident. In the past, I hadn't allowed myself to dress nicely. I hadn't wanted to draw attention to myself and didn't feel I deserved to look nice.

I was determined to change that, but the problem was I couldn't afford a lot. In the end I humbled myself and went out to the second-hand shop. I realised I wasn't too proud to do that. Besides, they had some really lovely clothes – some with the tags still on them.

Almost immediately, the compliments flowed in. "You dress so well," some people said. Others told me they couldn't afford nice clothes like mine; they were so surprised when I explained where I'd shopped.

Where you get your clothes from doesn't define who you are as a person. I hadn't realised that before. Suddenly, I was proud. I didn't feel any need to keep it a secret, nor did I live in fear of people finding out. I even completed a June Dally-Watkins course to better myself.

At first it was like putting on a very uncomfortable pair of shoes – the difference was that I got to decide whether I wanted to wear them or not. I discovered I could mould those 'shoes' to fit my feet. It often made me think of Nancy Sinatra's song, 'These Boots Are Made for Walking'. My boots were now taking me in a new and exciting direction. As I tried and tested many strategies, I also had the support of positive influences to keep me going forwards and not backwards. Wearing nice clothes and taking pride in my appearance helped lift my confidence and self-esteem and, over time, I came to believe I was just as good as the women I used to think were better than me.

As I expanded my horizons I met couples who'd been together since school. They'd never been with anyone else. I knew I couldn't replicate the part about not being with anyone else, but I figured I could explore the possibility of being in a loving and respectful relationship with someone who loved me completely. Watching and interacting with these couples instilled in me what a loving relationship was like and helped me realise that I too could live in the realm of 'anything is possible'.

My mentor and other members in the 12-step program helped me to see that my happiness was up to me and that I held the power in my hands for a better life. I finally realised that it had to come through me if I wanted things to change instead of everyone else having to change for me.

Boy, oh boy – didn't I want that better life! But it was essential that I continued to re-evaluate who I wanted in my life. An Alcoholics Anonymous pamphlet I read talked about being 'stuck on the merry-go-round of denial'. I could not afford to be with people who were on that merry-go-round. It was all about self-respect and not enabling the bad behaviour to continue against me.

I'd spent my life enabling the people around me to continue with their behaviours because, no matter what, I'd pick up the pieces and they didn't have to take responsibility for what they'd done. I enabled others to continue on their destructive paths. It was time to put the focus on me. Once I started changing my behaviour by not blaming, scolding or cleaning up other people's messes, things began changing in little ways for me. I found I liked myself so much more.

Slowly but surely, it was becoming all about me – who I was and who I wanted to become. I was developing a voice and using it to make people aware of behaviours and actions that weren't acceptable for me. I didn't have to yell and scream anymore. I could say what I needed to say once, in a calm manner, and then let it go. If I repeated it again, I knew it was me trying to control the situation when I didn't need to. Awareness became my best friend.

People don't know what they don't know. Some people don't want to change and that's their decision, but I wasn't that frightened little girl anymore. I wasn't going to disappear into the background. I no longer had to yell and scream to be heard.

When I was living with my partner, I was continually pointing out times when he'd let the children down by making promises and not keeping them. One day, after I'd promised my children we'd go to the beach, I heard myself say, "We can't go because your father doesn't feel well." He had a hangover, sure, but there was nothing stopping me from going out and taking the children to the beach. Nothing except me and my thoughts.

Since when did I need him to do something with my own children?

Since forever, but the thing was that I was critical of him breaking promises – and I was just as bad. It was much easier to see him doing it.

Once I'd realised this – and it was a hard thing to admit – I was determined going forward to always say what I mean and mean what I say. It's a value that I hold close today. It's my integrity. Your word is all you have.

I was getting to like this new me.

I was starting to believe I could be whatever or whoever I wanted to be, and I shared this message with my children. Nobody had ever told me that, but I was done repeating old behaviours.

Awareness is such a wonderful tool. Being aware of triggers is so important. Knowing how to recognise and combat negative thoughts is so important.

I listen to that voice today. Not tomorrow; right then and there.

Even recently, a really strange feeling rose up in me and I immediately said to myself, 'Okay, there's something I need to be aware of here.' When I sat with this for a moment, I figured out it was because I was doing something nice for 'me' by taking myself to the movies. And not just the movies, but the high-end movies with the recliner chairs and food delivered to you. I could have questioned my decision and reasoned things out and ended up at the normal cinema, but I recognised what it was and I continued. I had a wonderful evening doing what I deserved to do for myself.

Inside all of us is a 'little person' who holds all of those childhood imprints and wounds we all carry from the past. Being open and willing to reflect on my behaviour, adjust it and grow in awareness is part of my everyday process now. The fact I could and can do this is something that makes me very proud.

Over time it has become easier to put the focus on me rather than others. It was, however, a very hard habit to break initially because I could get anyone to feel sorry for me. I didn't know how to have a regular conversation because I felt like every time I opened my mouth, I'd go straight into bagging my partner, and that people would notice my behaviour more than his.

Now I can look back on those days with a smile because I've come so far.

The other thing I found I had to do in the process of taking control of my life was to step away from my family. It was simply too hard to be around people who still did what I used to do. As soon I stepped into their environment, I found myself being sucked back into the cesspool of very dysfunctional behaviour.

This was no longer my normal. I did not want it anymore. I wanted a new and healthy type of normal and, while I'd come such a long way, I still didn't truly know what 'normal' looked like.

Reflection 13

Growing up in an environment that taught me I was not respected or worthy imprinted those thoughts and behaviours on me for such a long time. As I reflect on this, I realise I'm the one who held me back from succeeding and achieving because I didn't believe I was deserving or worthy of having anything good happen. My thoughts remained negative until I decided to make that shift – not for someone else, but for me.

That is the one thing I truly struggled with – loving and accepting myself and believing I was worthy.

But I wanted more.

Then, I realised that to get more I had to do the work. I had to commit to saying 'yes' to me. I had to consciously change my mindset and the way I looked at things before my situation could start to change for the better.

I wanted this.

Over time, I started to not beat myself up when I got things wrong. I came to know that making mistakes was how I'd learn and grow. I started consciously changing direction. Every time something didn't work out for me, I directed myself down another path. Each path I go down, even if I don't go the whole way, brings something amazing to my life.

How wrong I was all those years ago – I do deserve more. I do deserve good things to happen. I can make them happen.

The first step is often the hardest – making the decision to change the way we have done things in the past, and being willing to do things differently as we step forward into a new future.

Do you want more for your life? Are you worthy of having, being and doing more? Are you ready to change direction? Are you willing to ride things out until you can see the benefits? Are there positive people to surround yourself with? Start with small steps – make a daily gratitude list, say positive affirmations, exercise, listen to uplifting audios. Begin to like yourself.

_____

You have the power within yourself to
make anything possible, you must diminish
the doubt and ignite the self belief.
~ Leon Brown ~

_____

CHAPTER FOURTEEN:
Self Love Lifts Me Higher

As I continued on my journey of discovery and came to know myself and who I wanted to become, I met the most amazing person.

And so began a story of love.

It really began when I decided to join a group called Mingles – single men and women looking for company in the safety of a group. Of course, a single mum raising three children on her own needs some adult company from time to time – and this was where I was at. Being brave, I booked a place at a singles dinner at the local golf club.

When I arrived, everyone was encouraged to 'mingle' before sitting down to dinner. I surprised myself by chatting with the other attendees and realised I wasn't that shy little girl anymore. I could carry on a conversation and, more importantly, I found I could walk away if I wasn't interested. I knew – and honoured – what I'd accept and not accept.

We were allocated to tables and seats that were arranged in 'boy, girl, boy, girl' fashion around the table. After a while, a guy arrived and sat down beside me. We got to talking, and as the night went on I asked him if he'd like to dance.

"I don't dance," he said.

I wondered why a man would come out to dinner at a club, knowing there would most probably be dancing, if he didn't dance. I started to doubt myself, falling into my old way of thinking. In the past I would've thought it was obviously my problem that he didn't dance. I also would've given up on dancing myself. But, out of the blue, my new way of thinking said, 'Fine. Everyone has a choice.' Hearing that voice in my head gave me courage. I turned my attention to the others in the group, enjoyed my meal and chatted with the other people at the table.

I also danced.

It was a wonderful feeling – not only the dancing, but the fact I'd taken control of my outcomes. I was stepping into becoming the person I wanted to be. I was becoming confident and sure of myself.

As I continued to mingle, chat and dance with others, this man eventually asked me for a dance. I was able to say yes because I was in control of me. I didn't have to punish him for saying no when I'd asked him – and I didn't have to punish myself. I made a decision for 'me' based on what was right or wrong for me. If I wasn't comfortable, I could sit down after one dance. It was empowering.

I got to dance with many men over the time I was a member of Mingles. It was all part of the process of discovering myself and discovering what I wanted in a man and in a relationship. At that time, it wasn't so much about 'finding a man' but about learning and experiencing feelings and emotions; ultimately, I was trying to figure out what I was looking for.

In Mingles there was a group of girls I got along well with. We made a rule that we all went out together and we all came home together, for safety reasons. If you found someone you really liked, you got their number and followed up at a later date.

There was one time I did meet someone who became obsessed with me. He wanted my number and I wasn't comfortable giving it. He then tried to convince the organiser of the group to give him my number. The organiser didn't give it to him, but that didn't stop him. He managed to piece together some things I'd mentioned and then turned up uninvited at our church to an event for my children. It scared the crap out of me. I asked some friends to tell him I was going back to their place after the event. I drove a number of ways home, just to check he wasn't following me.

It was a lesson for future situations. I'd been in controlling relationships and I definitely wasn't going down that path again. Thankfully, I didn't see or hear from him after that.

Today I wouldn't have a problem telling him his actions were unwanted and inappropriate.

As I attended more singles events I no longer latched onto anyone who showed the tiniest bit of interest in me. Those days of low self-esteem were in my past. The belief that people would leave if I wasn't their doormat was gone. The thinking and behaviour that always led me to disrespectful relationships was gone. I'd grown so much; I refused to waste time talking to men who were there for 'one thing'.

I didn't want or need a man who required someone to look after them without 'nagging'. I wasn't going to be the needy one, and I refused to live in fear of being left alone. I was an individual who had things she wanted to do for herself, and I was interested in finding a man who could join me on my journey.

So, back to the story of love. Who was that amazing new person I met? It was me.

I'd finally met this person who loved to give things a go. She was up for most things. She was up for having fun. And she knew she didn't have to include alcohol to give her the courage to step outside her comfort zone. She'd been there all along, and I was happy to have met her after all these years.

Since then, the new me has done amazing things – hot air ballooning, cave rafting, parasailing off a snow-capped mountain, tree surfing … the list goes on and on. The freedom and excitement of these experiences make me know I'm alive and tell me that all things are possible when you challenge yourself to do things differently.

Above all, though, I realised that I could never give love before because I didn't love me. I had to learn to love myself first.

Of course, like any love affair, this attraction did not happen overnight. Like any relationship, it had its ups and downs.

There were times I could almost envision two little gremlins, one perched on each of my shoulders. They'd sit there and whisper at each other – a never-ending dialogue of disagreement.

'I'm just as pretty as she is.'

'No, I'm not – men will choose her any day.'

'I don't care; I don't have to fit in with others.'

'I say that because I'm weird – I don't drink. That's why they don't like me. I have to do better.'

'I'll have to take the next step.'

'I'll give them my phone number.'

'I'll sleep with them.'

'No, I don't need to do that to be liked. It's my body; I get to choose what to do with it.'

And on and on and on they'd go. Until I decided to shut them out. Until I decided to listen to the positive voice in my head – even if it made me uncomfortable by telling me to go outside of what I knew and what was familiar. If I wanted to be a new person going forward, I needed to listen to the new voice in my head, even as it argued with the old.

'Yes, you can,' the new voice would say.

'No, you can't,' the old voice would whisper back.

'Listen to me,' said the new.

'No, listen to me,' argued the old.

Over time, the whisper that told me I couldn't change has faded and the whisper that said I could has become stronger. The old voice is still there but now I choose not to give over to its pull. Instead, I acknowledge the old voice because it is part of who I am but I know I don't have to keep listening to it. I have a choice and the tools of my programs and modalities are there to support me to succeed.

I also kept people around me who supported my new way of thinking. If I hadn't, I'm quite sure I'd still be stuck back in the days of my 'stinking thinking'. Back when failing myself and self-sabotaging my chances were okay. Still, those habits were so ingrained in me I had to work hard to overcome them.

At the end of the day, though, it is and will always be up to me who I listen to.

More and more opportunities came my way. I went out. I met people. I tried new things. And the whole time I had my new voice cheering me on. Sometimes, even now, I think back to the teacher who asked me what I wanted to do when I graduated and how I realised then that I'd never given myself the opportunity to think beyond the now. It's different today; I'm always considering my opportunities and possibilities. I don't let fear stand in my way. I have a fire inside of me, pulling me to more.

Why? I came to the conclusion that it must have been because I was now open to taking this new and exciting path, even though it scared the socks off me at times. I started believing that I was worthy of having amazing things happen to me. Down inside the deep, dark depths of my subconscious, something was trying to emerge. I didn't know what it was, but I knew its message was, 'You are meant for greatness'.

Back to my social group – Mingles. They were such a great bunch of people – very supportive and always looking out for each other.

One night, after a wonderful evening, we made the decision to make a real night of it – something we only did on rare occasions. A few of us decided to venture to another venue after the singles dinner to dance the night away. We found a table – it was a really long one. One of the guys in our group sat right down the other end from me. We'd talked a bit over the course of the night, but right now the time was for dancing.

It was a great night. I danced with so many people and got to know them a little more. During a short break, I saw this hand waving from the other end of the table. I looked up. "Dance?" he mouthed, pointing at the dance floor.

Why not?

Something sparked inside me while we were dancing. At the end of the song we sat down again, and I made the decision to explore our connection further.

We ended up laughing and chatting until the end of the evening. There was a connection there, on a much deeper level than I'd experienced with the others.

"Do you want to go for a walk along the beach?" he asked.

"I'd love to," I said.

We walked and talked on this beautiful moonlit evening until three o'clock in the morning.

Before we went our separate ways, he gave me his number.

This was something I'd never experienced before.

Someone was really interested in me. Normally it was the other way around.

I'd changed so much.

Reflection 14

What I'd learned by stepping outside of myself and embracing experiences I never imagined myself doing or having was that all things are possible if you know how to tap into your personal and internal power. Before gaining this knowledge, I was just existing. I was doing the same thing over and over, again and again, every day. I was living in a default world.

Science has proven there is a strong link between your mind and the world around you. If you know how, you can align your mind with the creation of greater health, happiness and fulfilment. It works if you work at it.

As I stepped further into this thinking, I was – and still am – truly amazed at how things happen or come to me with very little effort on my part. In the past I lived in fear; I wanted good things to happen to me so badly that I pushed and pushed to make them happen. In the end, though, what I was actually doing was pushing people and things away because I could only see things one way – my way.

Now I know I don't have to try harder. All I have to do is go within my own personal power and listen to that small voice; the answer will come to me. Every time, I'm blown away when my answers appear.

Life gets easier.

It doesn't matter what you are born into, we all have a choice of what the ending can look like.
What is your vision? What does it look like for you? It can be anything you desire. It is not about someone else. This is your dream and you can design it any way you like. It starts with taking that first step and saying 'yes' to yourself.

Respect yourself and others will respect you.
~ Confucius ~

CHAPTER FIFTEEN
My Soul Mate Found

We'd found each other in such an unexpected way.

After that 3 am walk along the beach, we met up again and went to the movies, drove up the beach in a 4WD – the usual things. Just getting to know each other.

Anzac Day was coming up and, as he was a Navy reservist, this commemoration was a huge day for him. On the other hand, I had three children to look after. I couldn't bring them with me, nor could I leave them on their own. "I'd love to go with you," I said, "but … the kids …"

He understood – he had children of his own – and I'd grown in confidence, meaning I didn't 'need' to go.

"Go and enjoy the day with your mates," I added. So that's what he did.

The next time we spoke, however, my intuition told me he was struggling with something. It just felt different.

"Can we talk?" he said. We arranged to meet at one of the shopping centre eateries.

He was there when I arrived and I could see he wasn't himself. I knew something was amiss. He bought me a drink, and when he passed it to me he couldn't look me in the eye. My intuition told me something was wrong. He was rattled and fidgety.

The old me would have gone straight to the worst-case scenario, but that wasn't who I was anymore. I was confident and wasn't desperate to have someone in my life.

The chat was idle. Trivial. Like it was the first time we'd met.

I let it go for a bit, but eventually knew I needed to be the one prompting. "I can see you're uncomfortable," I said. "Just say it. Get it out in the open. What did you want to talk about?"

Naturally I was concerned, but I was no longer that insecure little girl I was with my alcoholic partner all those years ago. I'd grown immensely and didn't need someone to make me who I was.

His eyes were downcast. He looked miserable. "I met someone," he blurted out, "on Anzac Day."

It was not lost on me that my lifelong fear of missing out because I hadn't tagged along somewhere had just been realised. All of my childhood doubts bubbled to the surface. As much as I'd worked to overcome them, they were still with me and always would be – the difference was my awareness of them. I could have let the fear rise up and consume me; it would have been so much easier. I could have allowed his revelation to take control and release me to self-sabotage my outcomes.

The thing was I wanted a totally different life, and this meant facing my biggest fear – being alone and unloved. Wasn't I worth loving? Didn't I deserve to have wonderful things happen to me?

My thoughts played tug-of-war inside my head.

You're not deserving.

You're good enough.

You're worthy of this man's love.

There were so many things to hold me back, but only if I let them. I had to make a decision for me; a decision that proved I respected myself.

And there it was … I was going to move forward, no matter what the outcome. I respected myself. I could see a life with this man – but only on my terms.

"What do you want me to say?" I said after several moments of silence. "We've only been out a couple of times and it's not like I've slept with you."

He was astounded. I suspect he'd been expecting me to scream and yell and get completely upset. But I didn't. The old me might have – not the new me. The changes I'd made in my life allowed me to respond rationally, to breathe and think through my thoughts in a calm and relaxed way. I was grateful to the alcoholic for giving me the opportunity to practise responding to unexpected things. It was like I'd had the best teacher in the world.

I respected myself now.

This lovely man was torn; I could see that much as we talked things through. I kept it short and to the point because I was clear on my values and I knew what I would accept and what I wouldn't. Reminding him of my standards and values, I then said, "You can't have it both ways but I'm not here to give you the answer. You have to make a decision for yourself."

It wasn't an ultimatum, but it was clear – the woman he'd met or me.

"She's engaged," he said.

"Well," I said, "you have a big decision to make, then."

I allowed him to talk some more and then I finished the conversation. "If you do decide to go down the path with this other woman, don't think you can come back to me as your second choice because that won't happen."

We didn't stay for long. He had a lot to consider and needed the space. Sure, I was frustrated, but I was proud of myself for being strong. I had an easy conscience. He, on the other hand, had a lot to think about.

The next day, he rang me and said he'd told this woman he didn't want to see her again.

It was so very different from the situation with my first husband who had chosen me because I was pregnant with his child yet continued to have contact with the other woman until she stopped the communication. I didn't respect myself back then, but I wasn't that person anymore.

This time, he chose me for me.

Or, rather, I chose me. I respected me. I wasn't desperate but deserved to be treated with respect – not a doormat for others to wipe their feet on as I'd been in the past.

I'll cherish those memories for the rest of my life because it was, honestly, the first time I'd ever experienced true love. It was the most magical time, and I knew I loved this man with all my heart.

And I wondered if, finally, the caterpillar had turned into a butterfly and found her wings.

Reflection 15

I met the most wonderful, loving and respectful man because I had changed. I attracted something so much better, and I deserved that life. If I had stayed on the path I was previously so comfortable with, I may have attracted another dysfunctional relationship, and another.

Thankfully I trusted and believed in the new Tracey, even when everyone else wanted me to stay on the path of the old Tracey.

I am so grateful that I followed my intuition and stayed my course for something better.

> ***Are you ready for change?***
> *Do you know what you're going to do to start that process of change? Here are the rules for change that I set myself. Which ones do you think you could action?*

- *Set some time each day for you.*
- *Don't allow people to speak to you in a disrespectful way.*
- *Be conscious of the way you speak to others.*
- *Start to question your standards and values and make sure they align with the person you want to become.*
- *Set yourself little goals about what you will accept and what you won't accept.*
- *Step away from people who don't align with your standards and values. Make room for people who do.*
- *Take baby steps to get you where you want to go.*
- *Have a vision and spend some time in that vision for your life every day.*
- *Know you are worthy of respect.*
- *Love yourself first.*

In the process of letting go you will lose many
things from the past, but you will find yourself.
~ Deepak Chopra ~

CHAPTER SIXTEEN:
The Melding of Two Families

This was the beginning of our journey together – it was as much about us being individuals and retaining our individuality as it was about us being a couple. The work I'd put into getting to know 'me' and who I wanted to become was starting to show. I allowed myself to feel my feelings, listen to my inner voice and trust my intuition – and it benefited the growth of our relationship.

It wasn't an easy journey by any means. We were melding two families – six children in total, ranging in age from eight to sixteen. My own three were twelve, fourteen and sixteen; his were eight, ten and twelve. All at 'difficult' years. Anyone who has done this themselves would know it's challenge. There are so many adjustments that everyone has to make.

One of the biggest adjustments was to do with values. Their family's values and mine were quite different. For example, I didn't allow my children to stay up to all hours and watch adult movies. We would watch family movies and that was the standard in my house. My children were taught to do chores as I was a single mum and I couldn't do everything. For me, that was what a family was about – helping and supporting each other. This included when we went camping as a group. My partner's kids tried saying they'd only eat dry packet noodles. In their minds, this meant they didn't have to be on the roster for washing-up duty. Together, we explained that whether they ate dry noodles every day or not, they'd still have to participate in the washing-up roster; that's part of being a family.

Melding two families with differing values is hard enough but having to contend with outside issues – such as a negative attitude from an ex – can make things even trickier. There were numerous little niggles, but a particularly trying one had to do with my son who had ADHD. He'd come such a long way since his initial diagnosis but could still totally lose it when provoked, and this eventuated one time when we were camping.

To their credit, when we sat down as a family and explained the situation with my son to my partner's kids, they understood. We gave them plenty of opportunities to ask questions. Family discussions were very important to us, however in this case it created an opportunity for their mum to construct this whole scenario where she blew everything out of proportion. She even stated that her children could not see their dad if my children were around because my son would kill them. Even though her youngest admitted that my son was provoked by the other two boys, she couldn't find it in herself to waver. Of course, this put their dad in a very difficult position, which I understood.

My partner stepped straight back into what was comfortable. It was easier for him to do what she expected, which meant obeying so he could see his kids. For me, your word is all you have, so I made him keep his word to her. He argued that his ex wouldn't know we were all together, but your word is your word – I was insistent. If we wanted a life together as a family, starting off with lies and deceit was simply not going to be workable.

For my children, the change in environment – the emotional environment – was possibly the most difficult. My childhood upbringing had impacted them, and they were very comfortable with the way things had always been. This frightened me and I was determined to give my children more. Not more in the physical sense, but more experiences. We did a lot of camping with friends. It was great being part of a group of people who didn't need alcohol to have a good time. We endeavoured to always make birthdays their special day – a celebration of their life – by allowing them to have their special meal, take a cake to school and celebrate with their friends. We made Christmas a very special day, too. I used to play the song 'Christmas is a time to love' as we opened gifts.

It was all so very different to the childhood I had. Everything came back to me wanting better for my children. It was my driving force and kept me determined to push through and do things differently in my new relationship.

My partner's ex was a constant challenge. She didn't want a relationship with him, yet it seemed she didn't want to let him go either. I realised this the first time I met her. We'd arranged to meet at the local shopping centre for the exchange of the children.

"So," she said, looking at me rather than him, "here are the children's things ..." Then she'd handed their bags to me and proceeded to tell me everything that she should have been telling their father – including the time they should be returned. It was like I was the babysitter, not the new partner.

Everything she said, every instruction, was directed at me. Once, I would've taken on that responsibility. I would have done everything she'd asked of me. But that person was in the past. "You need to tell their father," I said. I was calm. I also knew we couldn't move forward in our relationship until they'd resolved their relationship.

It's not easy for some children to let another person into their life, especially in a parenting role. However, I didn't see myself as becoming the parent of my partner's children. I preferred to see myself as a friend, but only if they were open to it, and in the early days everything went really well. Everyone got on famously – his kids, my kids; all of us.

Then, the 'honeymoon period' was over. The children had perhaps realised that this relationship wasn't short term but was here to stay. It wasn't one-sided. It wasn't only his children reacting; mine also struggled.

It sometimes felt like all our children wanted to destroy our relationship. They'd do things to try and put a wedge between us.

They definitely tried, but amongst all that there were so many firsts to hold on to.

Our first camping trip together amazed him. I'd raised my children on camping from a very young age. I knew how to put up a tent, how to start a fire and how to cook on a camp oven. And, what's more, my children were experts at it as well.

"I've never been in a relationship with anyone who has these skills," he said.

We were camping at Double Island Point. As a family, we'd go out exploring the sand dunes and generally had a great time. This particular day, though, all the children scampered to the top of the hill, and the next thing I know I'm spitting out sand. His children thought it would be funny to make sand-balls and throw them at me.

Calmly, I went down the hill to the water's edge to wash the sand off my face and out of my eyes. I didn't say a word. I wanted my partner to see for himself what was truly going on without me forcing it, because all that achieved was for us to have 'words'.

Another day, one of the boys, his youngest, wanted to sit between us in the car. My partner said, "No, I want Tracey to sit beside me." This caused a fuss, but we stood our ground. When we got back to the campsite, he refused to get out of the car to let me out so I let myself out of the driver's side and continued on my merry way. No bother. Nothing said.

His children tried their hardest to bait me and put a wedge between us. It didn't help, of course, that their mother seemed to be a big instigator in their behaviour. But I knew I couldn't change other people so I had to change myself, and to do this I had to look outside the box and explore all options.

As for my children, they were used to being able to easily manipulate the situation between my previous partner and myself, and it would always cause an upset that resulted in them winning. Now they couldn't because this man stood by me and supported me one hundred per cent. The children didn't have one person to manipulate, but two.

I did, however, have to acknowledge the imprints they'd developed.

The first time my partner brought a carton of beer into my home, my children reacted. There was a distinct sense of uneasiness. They seemed to be waiting for an explosion of words or violence like they'd previously been subjected to. They kept checking out this carton of beer, seeing how much was left. With my previous partner a carton would be gone in no time, but this time it was well over a month before it was all gone. I totally understood the fear that rose up in my children. They didn't know this was different. I knew my new partner was supportive and I saw him give my children so many opportunities and experiences, but they struggled to accept these things.

I envisaged creating this wonderful family, but the children weren't ready for this. Accepting where the children were at and keeping our vision of the bigger picture was crucial. When they had exhausted all their antics we could start to build that family.

Just like a sailor has to continually tack to get to their desired destination, I weathered every storm and got better and better at seeing the squalls before they hit. My awareness of these behaviours gave me forewarning, allowing me to recognise the signs well before the situation arose. We were united, my new partner and I, and together we were prepared for most situations.

Through trial and error we stayed on the course that was right for us.

All I could do was to put one foot in front of the other and hope things would work out in time. In the meantime, I just had to get on with life and focus on finishing my university degree.

Eventually, we felt comfortable enough to leave the kids and go away together, just the two of us. It had been nearly two years since we'd first met and now, finally, we were able to make plans that were just for us. To top it off, we weren't just heading off for a quick weekend to the next town or a few hours away, we were going overseas.

New Zealand.

It had to be New Zealand. It had been on my to-do list forever. He was keen to go skiing as he skied every year with his brother. I, on the other hand, had never seen snow. I certainly hadn't been skiing before. The only thing I wanted to do was go cave rafting; I didn't care about anything else.

The whole time we were planning this holiday, I struggled to believe it would come to fruition. Those deep-rooted imprints from my childhood, the negative thoughts, stopped me from believing good things could happen to me. I was taken back to a course I'd done, many years prior, at the start of my journey to change. It was at the Relaxation Centre in Brisbane and the presenter was speaking about goals – travelling overseas was one he mentioned.

All I could think when he said that was, "You have got to be joking!" Going on an overseas holiday was totally outside my realm of possibilities.

Even when we were sitting on the plane bound for New Zealand, I couldn't allow myself to believe it was happening. But I had to believe it and I had to believe that I'd created it. This was all part of creating my own story. A new story, with a beautiful man who loved me with all of his heart.

I'd done my research before we left. "Cave rafting," I'd said to him. "I want to try cave rafting." I have no idea why I was so set on the idea, except that it sounded exciting and I'd never done anything like it before.

We checked it out. "I don't know," he said. "It looks a bit like a backyard outfit."

Maybe it was, but I was determined to go with or without him. "I'm doing it," I said.

Of course, he wasn't going to let me go on my own, so that's how we found ourselves looking very glamorous, decked out in thermals, wetsuit, boots and balaclavas, with plastic bags on our feet and gripping a helmet and light each – ready to start our caving adventure with ten other adventurers from all over the world. We all piled into a van and drove out to the middle of nowhere where we slopped through mud, crossed a fast-flowing river and followed the guides until we reached … a hole in the ground.

"This is it," one of the guides said. "Now, please listen carefully to the following instructions as they are extremely important."

We all huddled in closer.

"There is water running through the cave," the guide informed us. "If we call 'flood', you must all link your arms together immediately. This is to prevent you from being washed away."

It was a pretty grim prospect. Yet, I was oddly excited. This was the new 'me' emerging. I wanted to be the person who was ready to step into this new life I wanted, instead of living in fear of what other people wanted me to do. I felt like something amazing was happening to me. My partner, though, was more concerned than

I was at the prospect. I truly, even in my wildest dreams, never thought I would step foot in another country, let alone find myself doing something like this. I was beyond excited. This was my new life. Having new experiences. There were times all of us in the group were a little bit hesitant, but we all loved it. You could tell by the gasps and the beaming faces. It is definitely up there as one of my favourite experiences, and to be doing it with a very special man who truly loved and supported me was awesome.

One by one, we switched our miner's lights on and entered the cave. Deeper and deeper into the cave we went. From one level to the next we walked. We went over an underground waterfall, floated on tyre tubes and crawled on our bellies. The tunnels seemed to go on forever but it wasn't that long. I think from beginning to end was only a couple of hours. Was there a smell? No. It was pristine, in its natural state. Sounds? Just the running of icy-cold water.

The water at the bottom was ankle-deep.

The guides led us through the cave system until we came to a waterfall tumbling down even further into the depths of the cave. "From here, we need each of you to sit at the top of the waterfall and fold your arms in front of you," the guide said.

Once we'd positioned ourselves, all that was left to do was pull our bottoms in and slide with the water down to the next level where another of the guides caught us and pulled us onto the ledge. 'Thrilling' is the only word that does it justice. It was like an out-of-body experience. I would never have thought I'd be doing anything like this in my wildest dreams. I just wanted more.

The waterfall went straight down. The guide was waiting at the next level to grab people on their way down. It was awesome.

A pile of truck tyre tubes was stacked up on the ledge. Once we'd all arrived, we sat in the tyre tubes and floated down the underground river. The silence and stillness were unbelievable. We were in an untouched world that no-one had ever entered – that's how it felt. How lucky was I to be doing this? How was this even possible for a person like me? It should've been a dream, but here I was living it.

I was doing something so far out of my comfort zone, and in another country to boot. This didn't happen to people like me.

"Turn your headlamps off," one of the guides called out.

We were plunged into darkness and silence.

It was disconcerting for barely a moment, then, all of a sudden, we were in a magical fairy land. Above us were thousands of sparkling lights – glow worms. It was beautiful. We floated down the river, relaxing and enjoying the experience for who knows how long. Time lost all importance. This was truly unbelievable.

And I'd said yes to doing it.

I'd challenged my thinking and confronted my fears.

I was loving this new Tracey.

At the next section, the guide asked if anyone had a fear of small places. I had no idea if I did or not, so I stayed quiet. What was I stepping into? Would I be able to handle it? With my new thinking in place I thought, 'I won't know unless I try.'

We ended up having to shimmy on our bellies through a series of tiny tunnels. At one point, I worried my partner wasn't going to make it through due to the width of his shoulders. My children called him the Hulk. He wriggled and squirmed and made it through – lucky because I doubt he would've been able to reverse.

From there, we made our way back to the entrance and back to where we started for a well-deserved hot spa followed by hot chocolate and scones. The adrenaline rush was indescribable.

We'd deliberately chosen winter for our trip for the skiing. My partner loved it. Me? I'd never seen snow before. When we first arrived in Christchurch we'd travelled over the pass in the middle of the night. The snow-capped mountains glistened in the moonlight. I was hooked. It was so beautiful.

The next morning I had another fear to conquer, another first – skiing. My partner was so caring, considerate and understanding of my fear of doing something I'd never done before. He was an expert skier and I was a beginner, so while I was having a lesson he'd go off and find us some trails to ski. He had more belief in my abilities than I did. I trusted him – another first, and another childhood imprint to be faced.

After this first day, though, we'd be at the ski area gate first thing in the morning and be one of the first vehicles up the mountain. One particular morning the sun was coming up over the mountain and the colour was stunning – it was all pink. Later, after we'd returned from our trip, I asked my partner what he thought the best part was.

"That snow-capped mountain glistening in the moonlight," he said. It was the simplest things that we loved about each other. The moonlight, the colours, the reflection of the mountains in the water – it was all unbelievable. He took so many photos – one that still fills me with joy every time I look at it is the one we had to climb over fences for, just to get the right vantage point to capture the reflections in a perfectly still lake.

"Let's do this every winter," I said to him at one point.

"Let's," he said.

We loved it.

Challenges and difficulties aside, at the end of the day we were both experiencing something amazing for the first time in our lives. I became increasingly aware that the changes I'd made in my life had led to me attracting the right type of person. Someone who loved and respected me and my decisions.

Did I make mistakes? Did I do things that I wish I hadn't? Yes, of course. We all do.

As a consequence of some of my decisions, rifts formed like huge chasms. They took years to heal. I was trying to find myself and had hoped my children wanted that, too. Sadly they weren't ready and, in the process, I lost them. If I'd known this would happen, would I have decided to step back into that messed up, dysfunctional world? Would I have rejected everything else that was out there for me? If I'm honest, the answer is no. I had to accept what was and move forward, hoping that it would all work out in the end.

As I reflect on this time I know I could've done things differently, but those imprints ran deep. I did what I did at the time and I can't change it, but I've definitely learned from it.

What I do know now is that we can't change what we don't know. I know so much more today and I have the honour and privilege to pass on my insights and wisdom to my grandchildren.

Above all, even when there were things outside of myself that I had no control over, I started making it my business to learn how to enjoy the moment, how to enjoy this day, and how to enjoy this life.

Reflection 16

What I now know is that I attract what my thoughts have me believe I'm worth. Once I started to believe in me and believe I could have more, I stepped into this amazing world of love and respect I'd never experienced before. It was amazing and scary at the same time.

Fear can hold us back from moving forward. It tells you to follow the easy road, but the easy road is not going to get you where you want to go.

I faced up to so many of my past fears in this time and I learned that it's not about making that fear go away. Because it won't. You need to befriend your fear. Acknowledge it and walk this path of success with it. Use fear as your guide to tell you that you are achieving and succeeding.

Every time your fears arise, it's because you're growing and stepping outside your comfort zone.

> *Trust and believe in the power in you.*
> *Do you want to be one of the few who go past that invisible line towards what you can be? Every time fear rises, will you have the strength and determination to say, "Not today. I hear you and I acknowledge you, but I'm moving forward anyway"? Do you want to be one of the one per cent of people who push beyond fear to see their possibilities and opportunities?*
> *Of course you do.*
> *And, in time, you'll notice it gets easier and easier.*
> *You decide what you want for your life and where you want to be.*

I've been trying to do the right thing for everyone but myself. But I think I've figured it out now. I'm going to stop trying to please everyone.
~ Emiko Jean ~

CHAPTER SEVENTEEN:
East Timor

The two of us just worked.

Whenever we could, we'd simply chill and enjoy each other's company. Bribie Island was a favourite weekend destination. Early in the morning we'd pack the car with the hammock, camp cooker, swimmers and the morning paper and head up the island's 4WD track. It was glorious. We'd spend the day relaxing, curled up in the hammock together. There was no need for that constant chatter; we were totally in sync with each other. Just being together was enough. We were like two young lovers. He'd cook us the most delicious breakfast, then we'd take a walk along the beach and go for a swim in the ocean.

Completely recharged and refreshed, we were ready to start the week all over again. It was so easy. We had each other's backs and we supported each other. One day we were talking and I noticed his T-shirt. It read, 'All you need'. I remember thinking that was so true because he was there for me no matter what got thrown at us from all the outside influences we had to navigate.

Our love would survive.

Weekdays were for work and family – I was now a high school teacher and he had his engineering company. We hadn't moved in together at this point. I was cautious because of my past experiences and he understood that. There was no pressure.

Things were tricky with the kids. They were at that difficult age. One of my sons was with his grandparents, my other son was at boarding school and my daughter lived away as well. Visits were rare and often tense. It was hard – not only did we have various problems continuously being stirred up by others who had their own agendas, but there were also all those childhood imprints to deal with. The imprints had no quick fix and I knew that. I also knew they might never be resolved because the individual has to be open to clearing them – nobody can do it for you. It took me years. I could justify anything to anyone, including myself. But I'd learned to do things differently and knew I had to wait for my children to be ready as well.

For a while now my partner had been hinting about marriage. "You know," he'd say, "girls can ask their guy to get married in a leap year."

He was a lot more eager than I was in the early days. It actually freaked me out, because I'd jumped in far too quickly before and it didn't turn out very well. At one point I spoke to my girlfriend about it. She came from a long-term marriage. "It's all normal," she said. "All couples go through this."

I wasn't ready, though. Not yet.

He persevered.

"Guess what I did today?" he said one day.

"I don't know," I said.

He leaned forward. "There was this couple selling their house. I went and spoke to them." He paused. "Offered them your house and some cash for their house." He looked at me.

I'd grown enough by this point to know not to react. Instead, I just sat there – no expression on my face – and waited to see what else he had to say.

"They declined," he said. "They wanted a single-storey house. Stairs are a problem because they're getting older."

I didn't have to say a thing. And I also knew we'd start looking for a home to share when the time was right. It would need to be big, though, to accommodate all the toys he wanted to buy. And it would need to have a shed.

Ever since I'd known him he'd been a reservist in the Navy. He told me once that he'd always wanted to do a short-term deployment but his ex-wife hated the idea. "You weren't in the Navy when we got married," she'd said. "Then you joined Reserves and …" Let's just say it's always been contentious.

In the Navy Reserve he worked as an engineer diver. There were compulsory short trips he had to do, but he really wanted to do an extended trip. "Just to find out what it's like," he said. It was always a firm no from his ex.

As I got to know him I began to understand how much he wanted this. He was so talented and could turn his hand to anything. People loved having him on worksites because he was so competent. He talked about putting his hand up for deployment a lot, but when it came to making a decision, he struggled. He was still scarred by his ex-wife's attitude. Scared I would feel the same way.

"I'll support whatever decision you make," I said to him. I was no longer that insecure person, worried he'd find someone else. "I'm not your ex," I added. "It's not my place to tell you what to do or not do."

Still, he procrastinated.

I let it go for a while, then one day when he was really quite down about it I decided enough was enough. "You have to make a decision," I said. "You have my support either way, but if you decide to go we need to know because we'll have to put some processes in place."

The look on his face was bordering on terror. "But what if you're not here when I get back?" he said.

I couldn't believe it.

"I will be," I reassured him. There was no way I could've known this, but I was pretty certain.

So, he took a leap of faith that it would all work out and signed up. Then we kicked into the planning.

Where would I collect his mail? How would I deal with anything that came up at his workshop? What bills needed to be paid?

Decision made.

Plans in place.

Off he went.

While the landing craft was refitted and sea trial completed he spent a period of time in Darwin before heading on deployment to East Timor.

We missed each other but found ways to connect regularly. Most of the time he rang me, because through the Navy it was a lot cheaper. It was lovely to chat on the phone. I'd update him about bills, the workshop and other everyday stuff, but we'd very quickly get around to talking about other things. Us.

Cards and parcels arrived on a regular basis. Clothes, jewellery, perfume – beautiful things because he knew I'd love them. I've no idea where he actually bought them, being on a ship the whole time, although I suspect he purchased them in Darwin and stowed them with his stuff to send through.

The gifts were lovely but it was his letters that filled my heart. Tender and loving – I absolutely cherished them and would read them over and over.

One letter he wrote still stands out in my memory:

Lone bird flying over, don't know where it is going and don't know where it has come from. No land in sight. I wish you were here to experience this with me. I love you and miss you.

He told me he was sitting at the stern of the ship when he wrote it.

I loved him with all of my heart. He was such a special man. So different from anyone I have ever experienced before.

"I miss your sexy ways," he said to me during one phone call.

After that comment, I didn't let distance stand in the road and found plenty of ways to have those sexy interactions with him. I'd send him a handkerchief with my perfume on it, or take nude selfies and cut them up like a jigsaw puzzle. He told me that when the mail came he'd disappear to his bunk, excited but never knowing what to expect.

I respected his decision … but I missed him so much.

Then one day I just did it. Something he'd been nagging me about for such a long time.

"Will you marry me?" I asked him over the phone.

"What?" he said. "Yes!"

So, there we were, now planning our wedding long-distance as well.

He was happy for me to organise venues and other details. "I just want to spend my life with you," he said. "Whatever you decide, I know it'll be beautiful."

Not long after my proposal, the phone rang. "I hear you got him to marry you," a voice said. No greeting. It was his sister.

I knew she didn't like me because I wasn't able to be manipulated anymore, but that response still shocked me enough to make me ring my new fiancé. "I need to know that you want this a hundred per cent," I said.

"A hundred and fifty per cent," came his reply.

It never really got any easier with his sister though. Probably the worst thing she did was to go running to the ex, telling her we were getting married and encouraging her to put nasty things about 'The Stepmother' into her children's heads.

The poor kids weren't given the chance to see that I wasn't trying to replace their mother.

East Timor was a real eye-opener – a war zone under war protocols. The conditions were very basic, and leaving the ship meant carrying a weapon. "A few of us went out to a restaurant the other night," my partner once said. "We even had to have our weapons there – for a meal." The diver's role was scary because they were the ones who had to explore what was thrown overboard by other vessels.

He didn't tell me much about that side of things but he did talk a lot about the children there. "They live such a simple life," he said. "Offering them a lolly – it's like Christmas for these children. They appreciate everything."

I knew it was hard for him not to compare these children to his own. Their mother didn't help; it was almost like a contest between the two of them, with the kids as judge and jury. It is hard to get kids to appreciate the effort and time spent on doing something out of love – especially when they're used to being able to buy anything whenever they wanted. Why would you want an old bike, powder-coated and rebuilt so it looked new, when you could go to the shop and buy an actual new bike for $500? Who wants to spend hours crammed into a 4WD and two weeks camping and roughing it at the beach when there was a five-star resort with your name on it?

Whatever he did was never enough.

While he was still in East Timor he had an accident. The opportunity to spend some time with the Army came up and he jumped at it. The Army vehicle he was in overturned somehow and he was thrown from the vehicle. When I found out I was terrified. He spent some time in hospital but ended up with just a very sore back from landing on the ground.

I couldn't believe how lucky he was. It could have been a lot worse.

Reflection 17

How often have you let old fears and reactions stop you or someone else from living their dream?

I could've taken the easy road and stayed in my fear, but I'd evolved into someone I now admire and respect.

I could've self-sabotaged the relationship, but I now knew better.

If I wanted this new future, I was the one who had to change the way I viewed the world and my surroundings. If I wanted something different, I needed to trust and believe it would all work out.

It was me who 'sabotaged' my outcomes by forcing change in the past.

What I now know is when I let go and stay the course of my vision, amazing things seem to happen.

Are you ready to trust and believe?
Do you have a vision of the life you would love? If not, what support do you need to work out where you want to be? Remember, you have the power. The choice is yours. It is up to you!
For me to change, I had to let go of a lot of the old thinking and embrace my new thinking.
I believe you can.

Being deeply loved by someone gives you strength,
while loving someone deeply gives you courage.
~ Lao Tzu ~

CHAPTER EIGHTEEN:
Forever After

After our first trip to New Zealand, I'd been hooked – on the country itself but especially on skiing. We looked forward to July every year, spending a week or two just enjoying each other's company and the snow.

All of our trips were memorable but one more so than the others.

Before we left, he took me shopping in Brisbane to look at engagement and wedding rings. We selected an engagement ring and he asked for it to be sealed up as duty free in preparation for our ski trip.

"We'll do this properly," he said. "The traditional way. I'll decide when and where to propose to you, so it can still be a surprise."

Obviously, it would be while we were in New Zealand, but that was all I knew.

We were staying in Queenstown near the Cardrona Alpine Resort, having hired a van as we did every year so we could be as close as possible. Each night we checked the weather report to see which ski area had the best snow cover, and then in the morning we'd be at the gate bright and early to be one of the first vehicles up the mountain. This way, we ensured we got the best parking area for a stunning view as the sun came up and turned the snow pink. We watched this while having our breakfast and then we'd be ready for a full day of skiing.

We'd be the first on the chair lift and the first to come down the mountain on the fresh snow. We loved it.

The plan was that I'd go and have a ski lesson while he went exploring to find places where he could take me off-track and support me while I was learning to ski.

I would go and have my lesson and he'd go off exploring. That's what he said, anyway.

One morning, about halfway through our trip, we took the chairlift to the highest point on the mountain as per usual. Usually we'd jump off the lift, ski around the corner and head back down the mountain.

Not this time.

He took my hand. "Let's go for a walk first," he said. "I want to show you something."

"What?" I looked at him but he just smiled.

"Take your skis off," he said. "Follow me."

I had no idea what he was up to, but it didn't matter because this was our time. We were at the top of the world in a winter wonderland and I wanted to savour every moment.

Our skis, now removed and shoved upright in the snow with the poles dangling off the ends, looked like some poor skier had taken a nosedive into the snow.

The snow was thick and deep. Walking was hard going, but it was worth every ounce of energy it took because when we arrived at his secret destination you could see for miles – the most amazing vista that I just couldn't tear my gaze away from.

"How did you know about this place?" I whispered, not wanting to break the spell.

He shrugged and pulled me closer. "A bit of research."

Cloud pillows were dotted here and there. Everything sparkled and shimmered. It was so quiet and so still.

I was stunned – to think that he'd spent time searching for this perfect place just so we could share it together was something I'd never dreamed of. And that's who he was – a loving, caring, supportive and thoughtful man. I'd never before experienced this kind of attention, and at that moment I knew for sure that I loved him with all my heart.

How long we sat there, I have no idea. Time seemed to stand still. The rest of the world and our routine lives were far, far away. We chatted about this and that. Trivial stuff. Random conversation. Just savouring the moment.

After a while, silence fell between us.

Lost in the moment, I felt him shuffle a bit and the next thing I knew he'd pulled out the ring we'd chosen in Brisbane. It was simple and elegant. The sides reached up to a single point with one gorgeous diamond perched on top, sparkling in the sunlight. Seeing it again in this environment was even more stunning because this time he was holding it, ready to put it on my finger.

"Will you marry me?" he said. "Will you be my wife?"

There was no question about my answer. "Yes," I said. "Yes."

He slid the ring on my finger and pulled me into a long kiss.

I was over the moon. I was floating on cloud nine. Every cliché about love and romance, that was me. We sat there in each other's arms and if felt so right. Nothing needed to be said.

This man had come into my life and scared the pants off me with his love and affection. Never had I experienced this. I hadn't known what to think, and now all I knew was that we were in love and I wanted to spend the rest of my life with this man, as he did with me.

Life was wonderful, and it was only going to get better and better.

It was my turn to live my dream.

Reflection 18

I'm so grateful that I had friends that were so supportive of our relationship. It was those people who became our support system. They loved us and were there for us.

I never thought I was deserving of such a beautiful love like this man offered me. I could've destroyed it because his children and mine tried so very hard to separate us, but we made the decision that our love was stronger. We knew our children would soon be of an age where they'd have their own lives to live. Why should we throw this opportunity for happiness away because they wanted to stay in their comfort zones? They were kids, we understood that, but we were both on a journey of self-discovery and this time we both had someone to ride this beautiful wave with.

> **Would you throw away an opportunity for love because others didn't want you to change?**
> *Do you believe you are not deserving of good things happening for you? What if you could believe your dreams would come true? What would that look like? Or are you one of the 99% of people who think it's not possible? Is it time for you to say 'yes' to your dream life?*
> *Explore what that dream life looks like for you. Say 'yes' for you. It starts with you making that decision for you.*
> *If it is to be, it is up to ME!*

You are forever and always the hero
of my heart, the love of my life
~ Anonymous ~

CHAPTER NINETEEN:
Tying the Knot

Everything was coming together for our beautiful wedding day.

My two bridesmaids and I went shopping for my wedding dress and their gowns. It was extra special as my daughter had come back into the fold. Sadly, my sons where not ready to do the same.

"You don't have a colour picked?"

My daughter was surprised, but I wanted to find a colour that suited their skin tones. It was fun because we spent the day trying on so many dresses and just laughing. Some colours were so wrong and made them all look washed out. Some colours were perfect but the style wasn't.

In the end, we chose red for the bridesmaids. Not a 'normal' bridesmaid colour but it just worked. Thin straps, fitted to the waist and a slight flair out for the ankle length dress. They looked gorgeous.

As for me, it quickly became apparent that I wasn't going to be married in white because it simply didn't suit my skin tone. However, when I tried a beautiful, beaded ivory dress there was a unanimous chorus of "Yes!"

I loved it and felt amazing.

Dresses, tick.

We had such a wonderful day, my best friend, my daughter and me, shopping and laughing. Relaxed and fun, it was better than a hen's night … and more memorable.

"You're hiring it?" My husband-to-be was surprised. He wanted to buy the dress for me.

"As beautiful as it is," I said, "where would I wear it?"

I thought it just didn't make sense to spend money on buying a dress I'd probably never wear again and, to be honest, I'd rather we spent the money on an amazing honeymoon. Despite being married before, I'd never had a honeymoon. It was all part of my dream wedding and I wanted something I'd remember forever.

My fiancé went out fishing with a few mates for his bucks' party. He was an avid fisherman and for him it was the perfect way to celebrate. Unfortunately the weather wasn't the greatest that day, but they decided the boat could handle the open water because my fiancé didn't want to just go up some estuary for such an important occasion. One of the guys apparently convinced himself he was seasick before he stepped off the wharf and, with the weather brewing, they knew it was going to be an interesting evening all-round.

They were right. After a while, the seas became so rough a number of the guys ended up in the bunks down below, not feeling so good. There was plenty of food and drink but a lot of them couldn't face it, knowing it would only come back up again.

"I sat at the top of the stairs," my fiancé told me later, "and told the guys that this was my bucks' night. The sight of them! I couldn't believe it."

Coming back in to shore was fraught with danger, and the waves were so high the dinghy being towed behind often disappeared below the white caps. It wasn't until they got back to the wharf, feeling much better, that the fun started.

A dear friend of mine offered to do our cake.

"Are you sure?" my fiancé said. I think he was genuinely concerned it was going to be some cheap backyard job.

"Trust her," I said.

He learned another lesson that day. "It's beautiful," he said when he went to collect the cake. "I don't believe it. Wow."

My friend had gone all-out. The cake was made up of two parts, the bottom being chocolate mud cake and the top, a bit smaller, the more traditional fruit cake. Smooth white icing covered both cakes, which were sat one atop the other and covered in the most exquisite, hand-formed roses. Small green leaves here and there added a bit of colour, and she'd draped around the edges of the cake with a marzipan 'cloth' that looked like it was casually hugging the cake itself.

Too good to eat.

The cake didn't make it straight to the reception venue – although it did get there eventually. It had to make a detour trip home so my fiancé could take photos of it against different backgrounds.

Another friend did my flowers. The bouquets were delicate and strong at the same time. Pure white lilies for rebirth and purity, and delicate pale pink roses surrounded by baby's breath, both symbolising everlasting love. It couldn't have been more perfect.

"Ah, the buds haven't opened properly," she said when she rang me that morning. "I'm going to try steaming them in the bathroom."

"Why?"

She explained that she was hoping the heat and steam would encourage the buds to open.

Who would've known? Of course, I had faith that it would all work out just the way it was supposed to, and if it didn't it'd be fine.

It worked. By the time she brought them over the flowers were perfect.

Everything ran so smoothly in the lead-up to the ceremony. My bridesmaids and I had a ball getting our hair done. The makeup artist was a bit late but it all worked out in the end. And when the photographer arrived, we were all ready. We had the loveliest time and I'm sure it was partly due to how calm I felt.

Nothing was going to spoil our day – not even his sister's decision to attend her friend's housewarming instead of her brother's wedding, or the fact that he'd made the tough decision not to invite his children because of their behaviours. It was sad and he was hurt, but this was our day and nothing was going to take it away from us.

Suddenly, it was time to go.

We were only about a half-hour's drive away, but it felt like the longest drive I'd ever had. Luckily, I had the company of a wonderful friend of mine who'd travelled up from Melbourne for the ceremony. This friend had stood by me the whole time I'd been estranged from my family.

It was such a glorious day. As we drove into the gardens through the massive gates at the entrance, I was reminded of the enormous timber log gates in the movie *Jurassic Park*. Like the gates in the movie, these ones also seemed to stretch up and touch the sky.

We were being married in the alcove at the gardens, surrounded by a stand of tall palm trees that seemed to be overlooking the festivities. I peeked inside and everyone was seated, waiting and quietly chatting.

"Come on." My wonderful friend, who'd agreed to give me away, put his hand on my elbow. "Let's do this."

As we entered the seated area, everyone turned as if in unison. All eyes were on me as my friend escorted me through the garden and down the red carpet, walking towards my new life with the absolutely gorgeous man I'd fallen in love with.

The minister smiled at me as I approached. He was a lovely man; I knew him from my church. It was uncanny – when we first met him we realised that he also knew my husband-to-be through the Navy. Somehow, it just felt right that he would be the one to marry us.

While my soon-to-be-husband was away we'd celebrated an anniversary of our first meeting and, somehow, randomly managed to choose the same card to send to each other. With so many cards out there, how does that happen even when you live in the same state, let alone when you are living 3,500 km apart? That's how connected we were.

Because of this, it seemed an obvious choice that our vows would partly come from that card:

I promise to give you the best of myself and to ask of you no more than you can give.
I promise to accept you the way you are.
I promise to respect you as a person.
I promise to share with you my time, my close attention and to bring joy and strength and imagination to our relationship.

*I promise to keep myself open to you, to let you see through
the window of my personal world into my innermost fears
and feelings, secrets and dreams.
I promise to grow along with you, to be willing to face
change as we both change in order to keep our relationship
alive and exciting.
And finally,
I promise to love you in good times and in bad, with all I
have to give and all I feel inside, in the only way I know how
Completely and Forever.*

As we exchanged rings, I had this overwhelming sense that this day was the start of what was going to be an amazing journey with a man who loved and respected me as much as I loved and respected him.

He gave me something I'd never experienced in my entire life – unconditional love.

Reflection 19

This was a new beginning for both of us. My husband said, "Now I know what true love is." I thought the same thing. Even though it was extremely foreign to me, I embraced it.

I knew I was deserving of such love. This man loved me. How was that possible?

I've come to love the person I'm becoming. I still have so much more to learn, but I'm open to the process. As I listen to my internal voice, it's my guide. It tells me when I have to address something. I don't dismiss the vital indicators telling me to pause and address something immediately. I recognise opportunities to reflect and I see if I'm drifting back into those old behaviours. What wows me today is that I get excited when my internal voice tells me another imprint in me is ready to show its face. I'm excited to get more clarity and to continue to move forward. I'm aware that pushing these indicators aside for a later time only harms me and stops my growth.

There's a lot I can do to help myself, but there are times when I need support to get to the deep, dark depths. At these times, I reach out to a fellow EFT practitioner to support me in getting clarity. I'm not fooling myself anymore, thinking that I can do it alone. Working with someone else helps me see things I can't – or won't – see on my own.

It's a health check for me.

If I want to grow, I need to take the necessary steps for my own health and wellbeing first.
What do you do? Do you believe you have the answers or know where your childhood imprints come from? If so, what stops you from growing? Is it fear of the unknown? Are you content with where you are? How would it be if you had the determination to continue to find out what holds you back from getting your dream?

I know it's scary, but it was the easy road that kept me stuck.

I believe you can do it.

It's truly up to you to make the changes in your life. I have to say, it was the best decision I've ever made for me. Do you have the courage and persistence to make that decision for yourself?

I believe you can.

Everything you want is on the other side of fear.
~ Jack Canfield ~

CHAPTER TWENTY:
Two Lives Connected Forever

Everyone was so happy for us.

Our guests travelled to the reception venue while we spent time with the photographer in the gorgeous gardens. There were little nooks surrounded by stunning colour and a huge variety of flowers. We had our first toast as a married couple together in this magical place with a bottle of bubbly my new husband and his brother had thoughtfully brought along.

Everything was perfect.

At the reception, my daughter's partner at the time kept popping up in the trees and at the table taking candid, on-the-spot shots. Looking back at them now still makes me laugh. One of the photos shows me, mouth wide open, about to take a bite of my dessert. It was the sort of dessert that deserves to be devoured in that manner – a decadent chocolate mousse covered in colourful, edible decoration with a wafer poking out the top. There are so many memorable images, all of which capture our happiness.

A wonderful evening was had by all.

We laughed and danced, and he even took my garter off with his teeth. It was also heartwarming to see my husband and his younger brother getting along – they didn't when I first met him. Now, his brother had just been best man and they were both as happy as anything.

The next morning we went for a walk along the beach with our guests before heading off for our honeymoon in tropical paradise.

Honeymooning on a tropical island in Tahiti was a no-brainer; we both loved travel and loved the water. It was the ideal location, but in my true style the time was also not without its hiccups.

It all started at the luggage carousel in Papeete.

We watched and waited as everyone else on our flight collected their bags. Fewer and fewer bags were coming out until … nothing. The carousel was empty. All we could do was fill in some forms at the lost luggage counter and head to our hotel with nothing but the clothes on our backs. In my case, it was jeans and a jacket because it had been cool when we'd left Brisbane. It wasn't so cool in Papeete.

The next morning we had to put our dirty clothes back on for our flight to Moorea Island. As we touched down, all I could think about was finding a shop – any shop – that sold swimmers and a sarong. I was hot and needed to get out of the clothes I'd had on for two days straight.

Once we arrived at the resort, we explained our luggage situation and the lovely receptionist contacted the airline to start trying to track it down. We also contacted the insurance company. "Keep your receipts for any clothes you buy," they said. There was a distinct lack of concern, which we weren't overly impressed by.

We were on a very small island. All of our clothes – including my sexy underwear – were flying off to who knows where.

Our first priority was to find something to wear.

There were a few general clothing stores. Swimmers and a sarong would do for now, but I needed underwear. Eventually we found a tiny general store that had some underwear, although it most certainly wasn't 'honeymoon-worthy'.

The following day we found out our luggage had gone to Chile. "It may take up to five days to get back here," the receptionist told us.

Never travel without a small pack of essentials. Always bring a toothbrush and a change of underwear in your hand luggage. Never assume your luggage will follow you because you just never know. Those are the lessons I learned then and still live by today.

Luggage issue aside, we loved our time together. My husband had been a diver for twenty years and he wanted me to learn too so I could go diving with him. I said "yes" and booked in for a diving lesson. I struggled with the instructor's accent. He could speak English, but his pronunciation was really hard for me to decipher.

I was ready to throw in the towel because very little he said made sense.

My husband came to the rescue again – of course. After the lesson, he took me to the water in front of our bungalow and explained how to clear my mask. My husband explained everything so easily and convinced me to keep trying. Eventually, I got it and we booked some dive trips.

It was amazing. Even my husband was stoked. The water was crystal clear, just like water out of a tap. Statues covered the sea floor and there were reef sharks and other fish everywhere; we even swam with stingrays. We got so close to them all. Wow, wow, wow. It was a different world, and I immediately understood why my husband loved it so much.

Another thing we did was hire a scooter so we could travel around the island and up the mountain. The funny thing was that we could have walked faster, going up the mountain, than on the scooter. All part of the experience.

During our explorations we came across a Tahitian black pearl merchant and my husband bought me a beautiful necklace – a dolphin with a black pearl attached. I still wear it today.

We got into the Tahitian culture. The dancing and the tattoos are unbelievable. Each tattoo has a meaning to the person who has it, and every tattoo had a story to tell. We just loved it.

On day five, we finally got our luggage back. Naturally it was disappointing, but we survived and, more importantly, we didn't let it spoil our honeymoon.

Back in Australia again we settled into our new home that we'd bought together.

The house ticked all our boxes. We had a vision of a shed and place to park the 'water toys' and camping gear. It had two storeys, with a gallery overlooking the formal lounge and a fireplace that would send warm air up into the bedrooms on the cold winter nights. It was also an acreage, which led to many discussions about what we wanted to do with it to make it our own.

I have a photo of him, taken as he was lying on the floor and putting together his stereo system that had been in storage for such a long time. He was so excited to have a place to call home.

It was the beginning of our new life together as husband and wife. We had so many ideas and plans for what we wanted to do. We loved spending time discussing what we wanted for the garden and how he wanted the workshop.

Everything was as perfect as it could possibly be.

Our time off went by so quickly and, before I knew it, I was back to my teaching job and he was off organising himself with work. When we got home each afternoon, though, we always discussed our respective days.

It was all so exciting – every little detail was as it should be.

Then everything changed.

Reflection 20

I would never have believed I was worthy of having such an amazing person love and respect me as he did.

Those who tried so hard to destroy what we had never had a chance, as our love was so deep.

We had a vision for our life and had accepted that some were not on the same path as us. Once we focused on our life, we stopped trying to convince others to join us. We decided that was their choice. We also decided to choose something loving and kind, rather than manipulation and games.

I'm not saying it was easy. What I am saying is that forcing people to do what you want them to do will usually encourage them to go in the opposite direction. I know that to be true from my own teenage years – the more my parents said I couldn't do something and put boundaries up, the more I worked to find a way around them. I recognise I tried to do the same to my daughter when we locked horns. I'm grateful that I continued to move forward and grow to a point where I realise some people are going to do what they are going to do anyway, so why waste precious time forcing people to do what they don't want to do?

The easier road for my life is to allow others to make their decisions while I put my time and energy into expanding my conscious awareness. I did that, and was lucky to attract some who was so in love with me.

What can you let go of to have the life you would love?
What is holding you back? Are you still on the merry-go-round to nowhere? Are you ready to step off the same old way of doing things and explore what is possible for your life?
Amazing things start happening when you let go of the anger, disappointment, hurt and all those things that take up your energy. For me, focusing on others and their unacceptable behaviour took my focus away from what I needed to change.
We all have a choice.
What is your choice today?

---

*You alone are the judge of your worth, and
your goal is to discover infinite worth in
yourself, no matter what anyone else thinks.*
~ Deepak Chopra ~

CHAPTER TWENTY ONE:
The Day Everything Changed in an Instant

It was coming up to the end of the school year and my husband and I were both looking forward to the Christmas holidays.

Our first Christmas in our new house.

I finished my day and headed home. Sick of the push mower, my husband had gone out that day and bought a bright red ride-on mower.

We sat down to catch up on each other's days, a cool drink in hand, then spent a fun hour or so with him teaching me how to use the ride-on. I was surprised how easy it was and how much I got done in so little time.

We'd both had busy days – me at school and my husband doing things around the property – and I could see how tired he was.

"Give training a miss tonight," I suggested. He was supposed to be at the naval barracks – a fifty-minute drive – for his usual session, and I was worried he was too tired.

"I can't," he said. "That's my child-support money."

"Let me give you the money this month," I said.

He wouldn't take it. "It's my responsibility," he said, then paused. "But I'd really appreciate taking your car instead of the 4WD. It's so much more comfortable."

"Of course," I said.

Thirty minutes later, he gave me a kiss and off he went.

As the night went on, I couldn't shake this unsettling feeling that something was wrong – I just didn't know what.

The phone rang.

"Is he coming to training tonight?" one of the guys from the barracks asked.

I told them he was on his way and the unsettled feeling increased. He'd told me he was planning to ring his brother on the way, so I rang to check.

"Haven't heard from him," his brother said.

I was beyond worried. It wasn't like him to say he was going to call and then not do it. I tried to remember what he'd been wearing and thought it was his Navy tracksuit. At least if there was an accident they'd recognise the insignia and call the Navy.

Nothing I did worked to help me settle.

'You're over-reacting, Tracey,' I told myself. 'You need to trust that everything is okay.' I couldn't. My gut wouldn't let me.

I paced and I worried.

I tried going to bed but I just tossed and turned.

Something was wrong.

My phone was on my bedside table. I stared at it then picked it up and rang his number. It connected, then from somewhere else in the house came the familiar tinkle of his ringtone.

That explained why he hadn't rung his brother but, as for me, I was none the wiser – and there was nothing I could do except wait it out.

Finally, through the curtains, I saw lights pull into the driveway. I rushed out the front to meet him.

Except it wasn't him.

Two people were walking up the drive towards me.

Two people in uniforms.

"Are you Tracey Walker?" one of them asked.

"Yes," I said. My mouth was dry.

"Do you own this car?" the other asked and showed me a rego number.

It was mine. "Yes, my husband borrowed it to go to naval training."

They asked if they could come inside. Sitting down, they then told me how sorry they were. "Your husband had an accident on the M1, near Toombul." There was a pause.

"Not again," I said. I knew what was coming before they said it.

He'd been killed instantly.

I burst into tears. We'd only been married three months. We'd only just bought a house together.

This couldn't be happening again.

The police asked if I would like to call someone. They asked if I wanted them to ring. I felt for the two police officers having to deal with this extremely distraught woman.

"No," I said, "I'll do it."

By this stage it was 10:30 pm, so when I rang my brother-in-law was already in bed.

"He's dead," I blurted out when he finally answered. Then I lost it.

Thankfully, the police took over the call.

All I could think was 'How could this be possible?'

He was never coming home.

My husband was gone.

Reflection 21

My second husband was the love of my life.

Even though we had only a short time together, we packed a lifetime of memories into that space of time. I am blessed and I cherish all the experiences we had together. There were so many firsts for me; for us.

My first overseas trip is the one that really sticks. Not really believing it was real, even as I was on the plane flying to New Zealand. Those thoughts of 'I am not deserving', and 'I am not good enough' playing in my head. It wasn't until we actually landed that I truly believed this had actually happened.

At our wedding, my husband was so surprised that everyone got on exceptionally well. Not having to deal with negative energy. We all had a blast. Very memorable.

No-one can take those memories away from me.

> *Our thoughts are so powerful.*
> *Are you consciously aware about what you are thinking?*
> *Are you aware of the impact your thoughts can have –*
> *on others and on yourself? It's okay if you're not aware;*
> *I wasn't until many years later.*
> *Start noticing your thoughts and body.*
> *These are the indicators that tell you something needs to*
> *be addressed. Definitely don't dismiss these feelings and*
> *thoughts because they will rise again another time.*
> *I know this because it was me that I needed to work on.*

---

*I know for certain that we never lose the people we
love, even to death. They continue to participate
in every act, thought and decision we make. Their
love leaves an indelible imprint in our memories.
We find comfort in knowing that our lives have
been enriched by having shared their love.*
~ Leo Buscaglia ~

CHAPTER TWENTY TWO:
The Dark Horizon

After the police had gone and I was left alone in our beautiful new home, reality hit me. I was a widow for the second time. I was going to have to face the rest of my life without him.

The questions came thick and fast. What if I'd insisted he stayed home because I knew he was extremely tired? What if he'd taken his car not mine? What if? What if? What if? The thing was nothing was going to change this devastating news. My beautiful husband was gone.

It wasn't the same as my first husband's passing. His death had lingered, drawn out over a three-month period. That was bad enough, but this time round my husband and I had spent a wonderful afternoon together and then he was gone. Forever. It didn't compute.

I know I didn't handle the situation very well. All I could think about was that I'd had this new future with a beautiful man who loved and respected me. Me! And now here I was again, alone.

Totally alone.

People can surround you. The room you're in can be overflowing. But the thing is, nobody knows what you are going through. That's where the loneliness comes in.

The voice in my head wouldn't give in. 'You're not good enough to have such a beautiful person,' it told me. I'd done everything I could to break away from my past, but I was still slapped in the face and mocked. 'You don't deserve it,' the voice went on.

We'd had each other's backs. He was there for me and I was there for him – it hadn't mattered what our children, our ex-partners or our families did to us and said about us, we were complete.

We loved each other.

We had plans. Travel. Home renovations. Growing old together.

Now it was all gone.

The most difficult realisation was that my husband's death, rather than bringing us all together, just gave the toxic members of our families more reason to come after me. I'd lost half of my security detail. Suddenly, it seemed as though the death of their father gave his children more reason to have a go at me. They did some really mean, spiteful things.

Being the second time around for me, people may have thought I'd be better prepared; more able to cope.

It's not something you can train for, unfortunately.

This loss was completely different to that of my first husband. This time we'd loved each other. Last time it was expected; this time it wasn't.

Everything had been pulled out from under me.

Why?

It was all so impossible to comprehend. Questions I will never know the answers to and deep emotions that would take time to work through.

It was like reliving a nightmare. We'd been married three months and the thought that I'd lost him after such a short period of time was not even conceivable to me.

'It's a mistake,' my brain screamed. 'They made a mistake. It wasn't him.' It was like a super-computer was trying to convert this raw information into sensible data but nothing was computing.

Our connection had been extremely deep, and I realised very quickly that he was gone physically but not in spirit. To this day I believe he has remained with me in spirit. Comforting me again and again in those moments of despair. He would show up in many ways.

One night I was lying in bed, trying to go to sleep and struggling. Out of the blue, I felt a weight on top of me. It was comforting but heavy. "You're too heavy," I said. The weight shifted so I could change positions and, once I'd done that, a warm comfort came over me. Other nights I'd have vivid dreams where we'd be just talking.

Returning from the coast one day, I became really cranky that he'd left me to deal with all his stuff and, suddenly, a car the same make, model and colour as his passed me. "You left me to deal with all your stuff," I shouted at it as it sped past. I was so pissed off with him.

The next minute, another car – again the same make, model and colour as his – was beside me again. This time I relented. "I know you'll always be there for me and that you're watching over me. I'm grateful for that but I miss you".

His car has shown up many times since then, whenever I've been down or felt like I wasn't coping. Either the car or our song. He'd given me a song by an Australian band called Leonardo's Bride – 'Even when I am sleeping'. We loved that song, and now it randomly comes on the radio whenever I'm struggling with my emotions.

He has continued to watch over me all of these years.

Some people might think that's weird, or even creepy, but I find it comforting. I know he's cheering me on and willing me to succeed.

Reflection 22

Paradigms.

These are old thinking patterns that drive us. They are a set of beliefs, feelings and actions that shape our current results. They are like gravity, and they pull us towards the familiar.

They're so strong, and most people are not even aware of how they shape our lives and hold us back from achieving so much more.

I made a commitment to myself to change my outcomes. To do that, I needed to challenge my thinking, because otherwise that fear would rise up and drag me back to what I was born into.

I had to make the decision that I was more than I was born into. I had to become consciously aware and recognise those limiting beliefs that were driving my bus in the wrong direction. It was up to me to change everything – the words I used, the behaviours I displayed, the way I treated my feelings and emotions, the people I had in my life. This took honesty and commitment to start looking at myself instead of at others and what they did or did not do.

This was an easy distraction, because while I looked at others and what they needed or needed to change I wasn't looking at myself.

Don't misunderstand, I still have these moments and I can still get caught up, but I now take the learning opportunity.

Today, people teach me so much more about myself.

> *It is definitely easier to fall back into old habits and take the easy road.*
>
> *If you are sick of doing this and willing to challenge yourself, then this is the time to take action. Have you thought about keeping a journal? Have you considered actively noticing your thoughts and feelings? If or when you do, you will suddenly ask yourself: Why didn't I see that before? Become aware of your thinking. Stop, be still and listen. The answers will appear if you take the time to invest in you.*

We can let the circumstances of our lives harden us so that we become increasingly resentful and afraid, or we can let them soften us and make us kinder and more open to what scares us. We always have this choice.
~ Pema Chödrön ~

CHAPTER TWENTY THREE:
My Soul is on Fire

I started off the new year at a new school, taking on a one-year contract for a teacher who wanted to try something else. I knew some staff because, as a student, I'd worked in the office before stepping into my university degree. The support I received from them was wonderful; the level of understanding about what I was going through and the loss I was feeling is something I will always appreciate. However, at the same time, I always had to be the professional and see things through – this is who I was.

I was fine as long as people didn't ask me how I was. As soon as I heard that question, those thoughts rose up in my mind and I was a goner. The tears would start and I couldn't turn them off. It didn't matter where I was or who I was with.

"I'd like to prescribe you an antidepressant," my doctor said.

I didn't see that as a solution. Besides, I'd seen what those types of medications can do to people and I definitely wasn't going down that path.

I'd always been the sort of person who searches for an alternative to pills. Relaxation music worked for me. When I went to bed I'd play it to help me fall asleep, and if I stirred during the night I'd just reach over to the remote and click 'play'. This worked really well because I could do it automatically before my brain completely woke up. It still works for me today. It stops the chatter from taking over and sending me down that rabbit hole where I can get lost for hours.

At work I was keeping it together as best I could, but when I came home it was a different matter. I'd be alone in this big house without the man I was going to spend the rest of my life with. An empty house where our hopes and dreams were replaced by questions with no answers. Was I being punished? Where did I go wrong? Was I not worthy of having a happy, loving relationship?

Even the one answer I desperately needed was taken away from me. Why did the accident happen? The accident investigation and inquest could not find a reason.

The loss of everything I'd ever dreamed of and the lack of justification for this accident was something I had to come to terms with. It's not unique to me – I knew that. It's a process everyone goes through, in their own time. There is no quota or time limit for the stages of grief.

In time, I decided that I needed to fulfil our dreams myself. I needed to action all the things we'd discussed prior to the accident, such as what we wanted to do to our new home we'd just moved into.

A friend came to paint the inside of the house. I also engaged a number of tradies to come and complete our vision of what we'd wanted in our home.

It took years to do everything we'd talked about, but as I achieved each goal it felt like we'd done this together.

And a tiny piece of me healed.

Reflection 23

The stages of grief I had to work through are the same for everyone: denial, anger, bargaining, depression and acceptance.

The difference is the amount of time it took. For me, it was five years before I really came to terms with what had happened; five years until I reached the stage of acceptance.

It still saddens me to think about what we could have had, but it wasn't to be. Instead, I have all the wonderful memories we shared together. And I know he still watches over me.

They say some people live ninety years and others live one year ninety times.

I believe the two of us lived one year ninety times, because what we put into the time we had together some people never do in a lifetime. I'm extremely grateful to have had that time together; no-one can take that away from me.

I've arrived at a place where I can look at my life journey as a learning. Maybe I'm still here because I have a job to do. Maybe I can take my learnings and challenges and use them to inspire and empower others to see things in a different way.

This is my new journey!

> *Many people have 'poor me' stories.*
> *I have many – hard childhood, cheating husband, abusive partner, love of my life taken. It would be so easy to play this story again and again; there are many people out there who would take control of the situation for me. Their hearts may be in the right place, but they don't recognise my need to stand on my own two feet and make my own decisions. Do you have a 'poor me' story? What are you going to do about it?*

I've learned … that our background and circumstances may have influenced who we are, but we are responsible for who we become.

~ Anonymous ~

CHAPTER TWENTY FOUR:
Lifting Up Others Uplifts Me

Five years of grief.

I'm not saying I was 'fixed', but I'd come through the cycle and I knew that now was the time to take all of my life experiences and use them to help others.

That child who failed herself.

The abuse.

The loss.

The resilience to turn something bad into a positive.

I've come so far from that child who wanted to sink into the background and not be seen or heard.

It was my time to step up, have a voice and teach others a different way.

I took some time out for myself. Time to regroup and figure out where to next. So, I decided to do relief teaching. This gave me the opportunity to come and go as I pleased without tying myself down to a nine-to-three job. It also gave me the opportunity to work in a number of different schools.

I took all my learnings from my childhood, my journey with my son and the resilience from the challenges I've had to navigate and integrated them into each and every classroom I taught in. I had a structure. Some students didn't like it, and that was okay because the ultimate goal was to help students succeed and not allow them to take the easy road to fail themselves. What I knew was it didn't matter what was happening at home; I wanted to empower students to take control of their outcomes. I knew that letting them get away with things was not the answer. All that did was enable them to continue to give up on themselves. I was not going to support that behaviour.

I set my course, and every class I stepped into had a structure based around the strategies I taught my son – that same boy who would've given up on himself if I hadn't persisted in finding a solution. It was about helping him to see that the power was within him, if only he had the tools to empower himself. This is the strategy I used in every class, in every school I taught in, for over twenty years – and it worked.

Sadly, schools come with a position of power – I am the teacher and I know best. This didn't work for me as a child, and I know it didn't work for my son because it just made him angrier as he saw himself being blamed for things he didn't initiate.

I understood that a structure of respect and courtesy would help all of us achieve success. For me, my goal was to do my job and support the teacher I was relieving so they could continue with their program without losing a day out of their busy schedule. For the students, my philosophy was that if they did the work set, by all means they could sit and talk to their friends or do other work. However, the bottom line was respect. Respect for the job I was being paid to do and respect for the teacher and the work they'd left for the lesson. That was what mattered the most.

I'd failed myself as a student because I didn't have anyone in my life who cared enough to put structures in place to stop me failing myself. I'd done it the hard way and I wasn't going to allow students to fail themselves on my watch.

Some students didn't appreciate my structure, but I wasn't there to be liked. I was there to support students to succeed. I had students who'd say, "Oh no, not her," when they found out I was taking them. And I had students who'd see me at the shopping mall and ask me if I had them next week – because they wanted to do the work and succeed. Both groups, however, were the same in that, when they stepped into my classroom, they knew exactly what was expected of them.

One of my favourite sayings is 'Say what you mean and mean what you say.' I live by this. Students knew that if I said something, I would follow through.

Everything you do in life comes down to looking at your own standards and values. Do you follow through in your own life? If not, then it's time to become consciously aware of your own actions.

When we lower our standards, we achieve less. You see it in school and you see it in adult life. It's the system; the system created and recreated by society.

The question is, what is the system creating?

Teaching is about empowering students to succeed, not about how students can answer questions on a test. It is about life skills. And it is about respect.

The strategies and techniques I used were subtle but truly effective. When I walked into a classroom I'd write a positive statement on the board.

"What's that mean, Miss?" they'd ask.

I didn't explain it. I wanted them to figure out the meaning for themselves. "What does it mean to you?" I'd say.

Everyone would see something different in the one statement, depending on backgrounds, upbringing, circumstances and situations. I wanted them to realise this. It's about self-discovery. My students started to look forward to what I put on the board every morning. One day I forgot and there was an uproar.

"Create your own," I said – and they did. A bank of positive affirmations.

Life is a journey, and planting small seeds in our students and children in the hope they will grow is an amazing experience. When you give people the tools and the skills to take control of their own outcomes, it is extremely powerful.

Everything changed for me when a period of two weeks at the end of my teaching career pushed me to the point of no return. I was bullied and intimidated for my standards and values that I had implemented successfully into my lessons for over twenty years, with support from staff. The system is not designed to get to the bottom of situations like these; instead, it's designed to take the easy road of blame. Once, it was my son. This time, it was me.

All I wanted to do was get the hell out of there and never come back.

Reflection 24

As a Life Mastery Consultant, I am amazed at how my clients begin to expand their thinking when they are given the right structure to transform their life.

We all have the power to do this if we are only willing to take the next step to invest in our own personal development.

I know that the deeper I step into this, the more I learn about myself to give me the best possible outcomes for my life.

If I want things to change then I have to change.

It truly is up to me. It is not circumstances, situations or other people that are holding you back. It is you.

You have the power, and it is you who needs to decide to change the way you have done things for years and years.

I ask you, is it time to say yes to your transformation?

If so, I commend you for investing in yourself.

You don't have to do this alone, because most people who try and do this alone 'fail'.

I know that you are not one to give up on yourself because you are reading my book.

Are you ready to take action for your life?

Start by doing what's necessary; then do what's
possible; and suddenly you are doing the impossible.
~ St Francis of Assisi ~

CHAPTER TWENTY FIVE:
The Impact of the System on Me and My World View

From that day, my life had changed. I wasn't coping at all. I was constantly on edge and the tears wouldn't stop flowing.

I was broken.

The students and administration had torn down my spirit. What was I to do now? I felt isolated and alone.

I spoke to a friend. "Apply for WorkCover," she said. We talked some more about it and she encouraged me to start the process.

I'd been through this process before. A student had gone to walk out of the room and I put my hand up to stop her. She'd pushed it out of the way, quite forcefully, and my hand hit the corner of the wall. With my hand swelled up like a balloon I wasn't able to write on the board, so they put me out on compo – WorkCover – while it mended.

This time, however, was very different and much more harmful to me.

The 'system' had a process for mental health issues that necessitated going to a counsellor or psychologist; one they'd chosen. This just added to my stress. There were no alternatives. You have to do what the system says.

While relief teaching, I'd also been doing extra study – something I'd done many times. My last lot of training was to become a marriage celebrant. This time, I was in the process of becoming a life coach. I'd wanted to take all the learnings from my life and use them to help and support people to recognise that there is a different way of achieving your goals and becoming self-aware. I was highly tuned in to my own feelings and emotions. As it turned out, I started using my training to support myself through what I was dealing with. However, when I was forced into receiving counselling I found the two were totally in conflict.

These counselling sessions were causing me more trauma.

I began finding it difficult to even see a student, let alone stand up in front of a class. I didn't want to leave the house for fear I'd be personally attacked by students. It didn't even have to be the students from my school, it was any young person I came across. I couldn't even go for a walk – what if I came across a student? I'd been through so much, but this was unlike anything I'd ever experienced.

One time, I was waiting in line for something and spotted some students. I was fine one minute, and the next my heart was racing. It was like I was about to faint; like everything was closing in on me.

I lost all control of my thoughts as they buzzed and spun and screamed in my head. I had the weirdest feeling that I was locked in a room – just me and the students.

I was their target and they were going … to … get … me!

I couldn't run. Couldn't hide. Couldn't escape.

Somehow, I don't know how, I made it back to my car. Then I sat there, locked in the car in the middle of the carpark as my emotions hammered me into a state of overwhelm.

How I drove home – which way I went and how long it took me – I have no idea.

It wasn't until later that I found out it was a panic attack. I'd never experienced that before and it wasn't nice. Nobody, least of all my doctor, had ever explained that this sort of thing could happen. I honestly felt like I was totally losing my shit. Like I'd gone crazy.

When I told my doctor what had happened, he handed me the name of some book. "Read this," he said. That was it. The system not only doesn't help people, it hinders them to get well.

It got worse.

A session with an EFT practitioner helped me understand what was happening to my body when I had a panic attack; the chemical reaction that was going on and what to do to calm my nervous system. But, due to WorkCover not acknowledging EFT as a viable modality, I had to pay for it myself.

Ultimately, though, I was forced to continue with the 'approved' counsellor. This sent me reeling back into my trauma. After every session I'd be down for days. Totally out of it. I was unable to be productive or to function in the normal world.

Soon afterwards, I decided that I'd only go to the shops early in the morning so I wouldn't bump into any students. I also stopped doing my regular walks – particularly at times when I knew I'd see students catching buses or on their bikes, going to school.

It changed my life, or rather I had to change my life to accommodate all of this.

Imagine for a moment how debilitating it would be to not be able to walk down your street because some kids were playing there. Imagine having to rearrange your day and only go out when school was in session. Imagine having no choice but to walk back into the building where your trauma started to hand in some essential paperwork. Imagine arriving early, before the students were in class, and being too scared to go in or even wait in the carpark so, instead, driving to the local shopping centre to wait. Imagine, then, a car pulling up beside you – with students sitting in the back seat – and feeling compelled to scrunch down into your seat and pretend you were reading or retrieving something from the floor.

This was me.

This was every area of my life.

The issue was that I was on this seesaw of a system not open to helping people. A system that puts everyone in the same box and believes one solution works for all.

I was proof that it didn't work.

Returning home after a session with the counsellor, I'd feel so much worse. Not better! For days I'd be 'down and out', unable to do anything. The counsellor wasn't helping – that much was clear to me – but nobody else saw it that way so I had to keep going.

Focusing on my studies became essential. This was the only thing that enabled me to see it would be possible to drag myself out of this black hole that the counselling sessions created.

The understanding and support I received from this lady – the EFT practitioner – was wonderful. Tapping was a way to clear the negative energy in my body first, and then to 'tap into' all the things that had happened to me in the past. It allowed me to release the hurt and disappointment losing of a job I'd loved for over twenty years which had been taken away due to a school system that doesn't deal with situations.

Now I had a tool I could use at home when I became overwhelmed. I began to see I had choices other than teaching, and tapping helped me deal with the times I did go out and happen to see students.

To me, it seemed ridiculous that I was forced down this path but I knew it was up to me to change my mindset and accept I had to do this process with WorkCover. I changed the way I looked at it because I had to survive this process.

It was a requirement and was not going to change, so I refocused. I put a lot of time into my studies while my head was in a good space and accepted that I would be in an extremely emotional state after a session with the counsellor. This gave me the energy to pursue a new direction for my career path. My love of teaching was everything to me and I didn't want to give that up, but I knew I couldn't be in the classroom anymore. Instead, I realised my new teaching path was to teach people how to take control of their lives, over and above their circumstances.

I refused to allow the system to keep me stuck.

My intuition served me well.

I trust in that today.

Reflection 25

The things I did to 'survive' were extreme. A voice in my head mocked, 'Adults don't act like that.' But they do. The way I was treated led to this behaviour. I trusted the system. I was disappointed; let down.

Now, I take the learnings from every area of my life – including this one – and turn them into a positive to help my clients. I love my job. In hindsight, I can look at what happened and think, 'If that didn't happen, I'd probably still be stuck in a system that doesn't support students and staff to do things a different way.'

As a Life Mastery Consultant and now an Advanced EFT & Matrix Reimprinting practitioner with over thirty years of life experience changing my outcomes for the better, I feel I can bring a unique element to my clients.

The fear that would rise up every time I saw a student shocked me, but until you've experienced it you truly don't understand how it is for someone else. I'm grateful I can have empathy for my clients because I've lived it.

And I've overcome it through alternate modalities, not mainstream ones.

*Character cannot be developed in ease and
quiet. Only through experience of trial
and suffering can the soul be strengthened,
ambition inspired, and success achieved.*
~ Helen Keller ~

CHAPTER TWENTY SIX:
Footprints into My Success

All of the challenges I've faced in my life have bought me to a space where I'm ready to face the world and be me.

I don't have to be liked by everyone.

I don't have to fit into the mould that everyone thinks I should conform to.

For much of my life, I've done what others think I should do.

Not anymore.

I no longer have to bow down to others. I am an individual with the right to make decisions regarding what is best for me.

Now is the time for me to shine and use my voice to break free from the restrictions put on me by partners, family, children, colleagues, acquaintances, the systems and the organisations.

Every time I step away from manipulative people, I take another step towards the person I want to be. In fact, I'm grateful for these people because they help me become a better person.

That little girl – little Tracey – doesn't need to stand in the shadows anymore. She doesn't need to be blocked, ignored or excluded. She is true to herself. She knows she is worthy.

Every day is an opportunity to learn and to grow. There will be bumps in the road along the way, but I believe in my journey and in myself as I expand my thinking and tap into the power that lives and breathes within me.

As I continue to walk along my path of self-discovery I'm ready to face challenges – that's what life is about. The difference today is that I know I'll come through the other side, stronger and wiser for the experience.

Reflection 26

The majority of people do not take the time to consider who they are and what their standards and values are. We assume we know. I assumed I knew and, on reflection, I just followed what I'd learned and never questioned anything.

In conversation with my daughter one day, she said that when she has children she'll raise them the way she was raised.

I posed a thought-provoking question. "What about your partner's upbringing? It may be very different to what you had, so there needs to be some thought given to the standards and values you both would like for your family."

For me, I didn't really have that opportunity due to the circumstances I found myself in. My childhood wasn't a great example for me to follow, so therefore everything was trial and error.

My long-term vision was only that I would give my children a better childhood than the one I had.

Having a discussion with my older sisters, I learned that when I was a small child my parents moved, and from then on they didn't have much to do with the extended family. My aunt told me she doesn't remember much about me and my younger sister. My guess is that's when things changed in our family, and possibly when the drinking became worse.

With a different way of seeing things, I'm always up levelling my vision for the future. I'm so very grateful that I have a process in my life to guide me through this new terrain, one that I live by today.

It doesn't matter what you are born into, we all have a choice of what the ending can look like.

What is your vision? What does it look like for you? It can be anything you desire. It is not about someone else. This is your dream, and you can design it any way you like. It starts with taking that first step and saying 'Yes' to yourself.

Let it begin with you!

CONCLUSION:
My Life's Quest for Change and Growth

My journey of discovery always amazes me.

The longer I journey, the deeper I go into the person I was always meant to be. It's exciting getting to know myself. The transformation I see from an extremely introverted child to an amazing woman who is open and eager to continue learning about herself is empowering.

I am always evolving. As I change, everything around me changes.

I can trust and believe in me. I no longer need or allow others to tell me what I should do. My inner power guides me to where I'm meant to be and who I need to be with. I choose to walk away from those who do not align with my values and vision for my life.

Intuition is my best friend. Instead of fearing what lies ahead, I embrace the future. I'm comfortable in my own skin.

I am deserving of the best life.

My passion has always been to help others, but I now recognise the difference between helping people and enabling them to continue their obstructive behaviours. The techniques I've created and picked up throughout my journey are in my toolkit – they help me, and I can pass them on to others. I have learned how to support the people around me without getting tangled up in their stuff. Empowering people to take control of their lives and make good choices is my role. This starts with my family.

Life is a journey, one chapter at a time. I don't have to read the same chapter again and again.

Today, and every day, I'm writing new chapters in my story. I know that if I veer off track I can bring myself back and notice what I need to notice about me.

I continue to try one more time every day because I want to succeed. I know I can achieve and succeed whatever I pay attention to.

If it is on the negative, it will be negative. If it is on the positive, it will be positive.

It is truly up to me.

My circumstances do not define the outcomes in my life anymore.

It has been an amazing journey, and I'm excited to see what else comes my way.

May your choices reflect your hopes, not your fears.
~ Nelson Mandela ~

MOVING FORWARD

I have started attracting amazing people into my life. People who support me. People who inspire me. I know if I decide to stay on this path to self-discovery I will create the life I dream of.

My vision for my life was very sketchy in the beginning. I was in uncharted waters, and at times it was extremely scary, but I have stayed my course even when I wasn't sure what the destination was. I knew there was more for me.

I put one foot in front of the other, believing the right person, situation or opportunity would come, and it has.

My journey and finally writing this book has been a vision for a long time and now it has come true.

I don't give up on my dreams today.

I know anything is possible, even when those fears rise up and say, 'it's not possible', or 'you're not good enough' or 'you will FAIL' or 'people will try and pull you down'. All of these situations can and do happen in my life but I have the skills and tools I need to see beyond those words and trust and believe I am meant to do what I do.

When I work with someone, I come alive because I am helping someone to build their dream. I love that I can I pass on my skills and techniques to my grandchildren. I wish I had these same early experiences with my children, but I was learning how to implement those skills and techniques into my life back then. I have to be grateful that I get to share my knowledge to help them see the world in a totally different way now.

My heart is so full of love for those I help.

All of my learnings along the way, the things I learned from tapping into those deeply rooted paradigms that held me back for so long, will always be there. It's how I respond to them that matters.

Changing my thoughts in those moments is empowering, and I love to look them in the eye and say, 'not today'. Making decisions for my life today is my choice.

I can go down the rabbit hole of the past if I choose but I've come too far to even consider doing that now. I'm a totally different person. I can walk into a room and know that I am worthy.

We all come across people who want to pull us down; it's inevitable. But, we all have a choice.

Today, I choose ME.

Ingram Content Group Australia Pty Ltd
Printed in Australia
AUHW020939260623
379949AU00009B/9